Once more unto the Breach

Managing information security in an uncertain world

Second edition

Once more unto the Breach

Managing information security in an uncertain world

Second edition

ANDREA C SIMMONS

IT Governance Publishing

IT Governance Publishing
IT Governance Limited
Unit 3, Clive Court
Bartholomew's Walk
Cambridgeshire Business Park
Ely, Cambridgeshire
CB7 4EA
United Kingdom
www.itgovernance.co.uk

First published in the United Kingdom in 2012
by IT Governance Publishing: ISBN 978-1-84928-388-5

Second edition published in 2015

ISBN: 978-1-84928-708-1

PREFACE

This book was first spawned from years of experience in the UK information security industry, both from being in the role of an information security manager and more recently a chief information security officer, and from observing many individuals adopting the role from a standing start, without making a deliberate career choice or realising that it would be part of their role. Let's be honest, you don't hear many (any?) teenagers planning to leave school to be an information security manager! The role is often 'gifted' (in the poisoned chalice sense!) to an individual on top of their existing, hugely busy, day job, because the person handing over the 'gift' does not understand the breadth of what is required. Therefore, the individual in receipt of the 'gift' is not afforded the time or respect required either to provide appropriate advice and guidance for the protection of information assets belonging to the organisation in question, nor to actively encourage colleagues to do likewise.

The aim of this book is to provide a 'coalface' view of what tackling this role actually looks like in action, drawn from my own experience; having spent a year during my PhD studies taking on the role of information security manager for a UK public sector body, I quickly realised the benefit of keeping copious notes! In academic circles, this is known as carrying out 'participant observation' and was done as part of PhD research into embedding best-practice information assurance. The author observed a great many incidents, events and risks, and also participated in innovative solution creation in order to address all of these.

Preface

The results of this study are worth putting together in this tome - almost every day brought with it a little gem which, if you were not 'in tune' with the wondrous breadth of information security, you might have missed, including the cause and the potential mitigation and 'lessons-learned' elements.

This book is effectively written through the spectrum of the 'project lessons learned', which were harshly, but fairly, created after phase one of a long project. Given that this book is based on a real project that took place several years ago, the text is imbued with a great deal of hindsight. However, these lessons could no doubt have been written by many people in any organisation. Part of the author's current research has been looking into the whys and wherefores of how organisations create lessons-learned logs, but do not actually learn the lessons well nor implement the required changes in practices. The work is appropriately anonymised.

While some of these issues and incidents took place between 2009 and 2011 and may feel out of date (given how fast the pace of life is in the information age), you may still be experiencing some of them and the lessons learned will hold true for most situations.

So, I share this with you in the hope that either they will resonate with you and you will feel reassured that you are not insane, or you will start to see things differently and know what to watch out for in the future with enhanced vision.

ABOUT THE AUTHOR

Andrea Simmons, M.Inst.ISP, CISSP, CISM, FBCS CITP, MA, ISSA Senior Member and IISP Director, is Chief Information Security Officer for HP Enterprise Services.

Andrea is an enthusiastic information governance evangelist and specialist with extensive experience in both the private sector and the UK-wide public sector – including local government, non-departmental public bodies (NDPBs), and health and emergency services. Andrea has expertise in information security management systems (ISMSs) (ISO27001, strategy and planning, policies and procedures development and implementation, etc.), information rights legislation/regulation and standards (including data protection (DP) and freedom of information (FOI)), records management (RM), governance risk and compliance (GRC), information assurance (IA), business continuity planning (BCP), resilience and disaster recovery. This covers the breadth of UK public and private sector compliance requirements including ISO27001, FSA, ICO, data handling, PCI, CoCo, GCx, security architecture and design, implementing compliance programmes and ISMSs, through the deliverance of change management programmes and innovative training solutions, while being heavily influenced by US and global legislation, regulation and standards development and maturation. Andrea has been an active information security industry contributor for a decade, writing articles and blogs and presenting at conferences, seminars and workshops.

Andrea has contributed to standards developments and industry research and is now working on a PhD in information assurance through the University of Wolverhampton, researching the background to the development of the subject itself – its genus and meaning across the industry – and tackling the language barriers created by our complex web of industry acronyms and misconstrued meanings, which appear to be hampering the implementation of best-practice information assurance in the context of the information society.

Andrea has also held the role of consultant security forum manager for the BCS Chartered Institute of IT: *www.bcs.org/security* and is now a member of the BCS Security Community of Expertise (SCoE), and has been a member of the Management Committee of IAAC, *www.iaac.org.uk*, for several years. She is also a full, Chartered Fellow of the BCS and its relevant specialist groups: security, audit and law, and is on the BCS Register of Security Experts. Andrea is also a member of ISACA, ISSA, ISC2 and a founding member of the Institute of Information Security Professionals, to name but a few!

Andrea achieved Chartered IT Professional Status in February 2007 and M.Inst.ISP in 2008. In January 2012, Andrea was awarded Senior Member status of the ISSA, *www.issa.org/*.

ACKNOWLEDGEMENTS

I am indebted to my parents for bringing me up with the strength of character that has made me a relatively open individual, which means that people tend to warm to me, rather than shying away. This can be a helpful trait in the role of information security manager, as you need people to feel that they can trust you and can share whatever issues are taking place that need solutions. I am also grateful to my mother, Jean, most particularly for a love of language and the spoken word – and even more so that she would take the time to read this book, so utterly 'out of the norm' from her normal reading, and find all the little niggles that needed to be ironed out!

I am grateful to all those colleagues I have met in the various roles in which I have been lucky enough to have influence during the last two decades. There really are some fascinating jobs out there, but more interesting yet, from our perspective, has to be how to weave information security into the fabric of what we are doing, to make it live and breathe on a daily basis.

I am also indebted to the various colleagues I have met along the way – in particular, those who are as keen to change things for the good as I am – dedicated to representing information security positively, rather than negatively; sadly, the usual default position. We don't have to be 'the department of no'!

Last, but by no means least, I am, of course, hugely grateful to my husband for putting up with my continuous need to write stuff down!

Acknowledgements

We would like to acknowledge the following reviewers of this book for their useful contributions: Chris Evans DPSM MBCS and Giuseppe G. Zorzino CISA CGEIT CRISC, Lead Auditor 27001, Security Architect.

CONTENTS

Contents

IA profession. Health warning – I should say up front that this book won't pull any punches.

When this book originally came out, it focused on a period of time between 2009 and 2011. In many media reviews of the time 2011 was hailed as the year of the hacker, in terms of the volume of media coverage and, therefore, widespread global awareness, and was noted to be a year of significant data breaches and losses because of the large numbers of individuals directly affected or impacted. Today we regularly see reports of well-known companies falling victim to cyber attacks, and the situation that seemed exceptional in 2011 has become the norm. In fact, given the volume of breaches experienced since this book was first published, its contents have never been more accurate or more appropriate. 2014 in particular was a year of extreme activity, with vulnerability after vulnerability being experienced across all operating systems – including the first significant chink in the armour of all things *nix (with the Bourne Again Shell – BASH/Shellshock vulnerability). In reality, the breaches that are covered by the media are only the tip of the iceberg, and the longer you work in the industry the clearer this becomes.

Beneath the story reported by the media there is usually a

Security is having a bad decade.....
So many breaches!
10/2014: Home Depot (53m records)
9/2014: Home Depot (56m cards)
8/2014: JPMorgan Chase (83m records)
6/2014: iCloud (celebrity 'hacking')
5/2014: eBay (145m records)
12/2013: Target (110m records)
10/2013: Adobe (152m records)
And on, and on … It's obvious there are some serious issues to be addressed.

---

raft of information security-based failings that have been present for quite some time.

All of these, one after the other, like multiple buses arriving at the same time, could have been adequately resolved with three key information security management tenets, which are addressed through this book:

1. Inventory management (knowing what you have) [Chapters 1, 4, 7 and 8]

2. Patch management (keeping it up to date) [Chapter 2]

3. Vulnerability management (protecting it from harm) [Chapter 3]

Why is this the case, given that there are likely to have been many valid audit reports containing reference to issues that needed to be addressed? Indeed, there is no doubt that had recommendations been adhered to in these cases, risk reduction would have occurred and the number of breaches would equally have been lessened. It seems to me that, as a society, we have seen a greater shift in recent times towards openness and transparency in all walks of life and across all levels of leadership. I believe we should be following this trend in our own industry.

This book is an insider's view of how many actual breaches (often seen as incidents) are going on all the time, but which do not get reported, either internally or externally. The educational point of the book is to reframe what it actually means to be an ISM, as well as what is meant by an incident, how we respond to it and what the most appropriate reporting and reactions should be. We will do this through the old art of storytelling, in the hope that better informed and more aware ISMs will be able to provide much greater protection to their organisations and their information assets.

The book will be peppered with references to real issues, conflicts and conundrums that ISMs constantly have to deal with, and I hope that it will shed light on possible solutions and pragmatic ways forward. It should be usable as a learning device and reference guide.

The chapter structure is based on a 12-month chronology, running from August to July.

August – pulling a team together. As a project manager in information security you get what you are given and you have to make the best of it, so you have to enthuse those around you regarding your goals while explaining the changes in behaviour expected and what the end game looks like.

September – street trash. This chapter is centred on an event that may remind you of those times when you read news stories and don't expect them to happen to you. But when you spot the blindingly obvious, always remember to take a photo so you have the evidence to 'show and tell', following the mantra 'a picture is worth a thousand words'.

October – compliance is only skin deep. Once you've completed an audit, in whatever shape or form, following a 'tick box' exercise is no good if you can't back it up with evidence. Now starts the hard work of living by your word.

November – how remote is remote? Identifying home-workers and remote workers can be a tricky business depending on your partners and your boundaries, the competing requirements of each, and conflicting legislative and standard requirements.

December – oh, for the sake of yet another proposal. A large project involves much more than just dealing with the actual security controls which must be implemented. Battling with politics and management can be hugely time-consuming and diverting.

January – a battle won. While the project politics game can be won in the end and you've got your budget, you still need to manage it tightly and closely before everyone else wants to get their hands on it and get their pet projects funded!

February – money doesn't buy happiness: 'twas ever thus. While the financial resources are available, it can be difficult to apportion them appropriately and spend them in time, particularly in the public sector. And if you don't spend them, you run the risk of losing them, which is a shame when you have worked so hard to get them in the first place!

March – slipping through the net. When working in local government, you are only a small part of a much larger picture. The links with central government can be strong or weak, depending on your position. An impending election puts a significant, nationwide embargo on spend and project completion seems further and further away. And to top it all off, there is a virus outbreak. So what do you do when malware strikes? A Conficker infection runs the risk of doing some significant network damage and any publicity needs to be very carefully handled.

April – linking InfoSec with InfoGov. In order to arrange some level of succession management, it is important to arrange for the right players to work together to deliver a more holistic solution for the organisation. This has always been the case, but takes on a new meaning, given the changing political landscape.

May – politics and management. Situational awareness is an important element of your role and you need to be aware of the bigger picture in which you are operating, as an organisation, in order to maintain appropriate information security.

June – what the auditors shouldn't know. Following a significant review of laptop usage across the organisation, it was found that the costs and likely level of breach to the organisation were huge if one was to be lost or stolen, given their current unencrypted status. But a senior management team thought it best to 'bury the bad news'.

July – so near and yet so far. Following the election of the new government, and in line with many public sector cuts and project closures, the project management role was let go and it was time to walk away.

Throughout the book, there are breakout sections referencing events that have occurred or thoughts that have arisen as a result of things people have said which provided inspiration to the author. There is also what will appear to be a great deal of repetition – but this is exactly the reality of the job as an ISM. Life in the trenches is one long exercise of doing the same things over and over again but with nuances, and with superior solutions as you get to know the organisation, its culture and what works. The tasks don't stop – hence security is a process not a project!

The job of the ISM is to consider everything in terms of the potential risks to the organisation and to seek to implement appropriate preventative or deterrent controls in due course. The role is never-ending, as there are always new employees that need to be embraced into the culture of your organisation and who need to understand their responsibilities and the requirements placed upon them in terms of protection of information assets.

Being an ISM is about being both a counsellor for many and a change activist for your organisation. There is a level of inspiration required for you to do what needs to be done, given that the historical view of the role and its positioning has not necessarily been entirely positive. I hope that this book goes some way to changing this impression for the better.

Consumerisation will no doubt be featuring large for many organisations as part of 'the three Cs' of Cyber, Consumerisation and Cloud that have dominated the conversation in recent years. This is now more commonly known as 'bring your own device' (BYOD) and presents significant challenges to ICT departments in terms of estate management and the incorporation of different operation platforms alongside existing corporate systems. This book is not designed to address these issues, as there is a growing number of resources available to do so. Suffice to say that, from an information security point of view, the task in hand is still to protect information assets. This requires controls and safeguards, and consideration of all aspects of confidentiality, integrity and availability.

CHAPTER 1: AUGUST - PULLING A TEAM TOGETHER

It's not a project ...

The most important thing to remember from this book may very well be that there should be no more information security projects, but rather programmes. What we, as information security professionals, are ultimately delivering are programmes of change across our organisations. All the security breaches that have dogged the second decade of the 21st century appear to have been as a result of operating at odds with the importance of the key elements of security (i.e. maintaining the integrity, confidentiality and availability of information assets). This book will not repeat detailed definitions of information security per se – there are many, many resources available out there to do just that. In particular, the reader is referred to the 10 domains of the common body of knowledge (CBK) for information security, maintained by the International Information Systems Security Certification Consortium ((ISC)^2). But for the sake of clarity, here is a quick reminder of what are considered to be information assets.

Information assets include:

- paper-based systems and hard-copy reports
- telephone conversations and instant messages
- internal and external post
- information on fax machines and printers
- information on laptops and palmtops
- information on hard drives of all sorts, including stateless
- information stored on CDs, USBs, DVDs, disks and tapes
- information on servers and workstations
- information transmitted over networks.

This book is designed for a readership that appreciates operating in a paradigm that knows and understands something of the expectations of information security – i.e. that the task at hand is very much more about the people and the processes involved in information asset protection than it is about the information technology used to support these. In fact, it is often the case that the ISM is not a technical expert in any of the technologies being used, or intended to be deployed, across the network of the organisation for which they are providing security advice. The ISM needs to know about the requirements and how best to achieve them, and to understand all sorts of peripheral issues, rather than the specifics of each and every technology. It simply isn't possible, and in many cases, this is why it is necessary to have IT security administrators, security architects and many other roles, as well as the ISM – i.e. the responsibility should not rest on just one individual.

While it is true that the role and its functions started out in technology, as data security has matured into information security the skills and role profile have matured too. For an organisation to benefit from the possible outcomes of dealing with the plethora of information-related challenges being faced on a daily basis, the ISM role needs to be one with a broader reach and a broader skill set.

So, the idea in these chapters is to provide an insider's view of what it is really like to operate as an ISM, in a real organisation dealing with everyday challenges. By using the role of 'project manager' on a programme of change we will highlight all the various incidents and issues that arise on an almost daily basis – many of which often go unnoticed. Consider reading this book as the equivalent of a training ground of things to watch out for, in case you ever find yourself blinkered and starting to miss the smaller things. This is very much akin to missing the flapping of the proverbial butterfly wing and, thus, not spotting the fact that a storm is coming down on you, as a result of having missed the small detail earlier on.

When you are set the task of delivering a particular project, your team members will always be a significant part of the success or failure of that project. One of the key failures of security change management is that it is perceived as a project, and, thus, by its very nature is assumed to have a beginning, middle and an end. In reality, security is something that needs to be baked into an organisation and, thus, embedded into its fabric – and because of this, it lends itself more to a programme than a project because there is no real end to these activities; security will ultimately be constantly changing in order to adapt to the information risks that present themselves along the journey.

When an organisation has a project focus all of the time, it seems that there are 'meetings about meetings' plus project plans and reports to be maintained constantly, usually at the expense of doing the actual job that needs to be done. It's a very difficult path to be negotiated, between playing the political animal and delivering on the requirements of the job. It is better if the ISM stays focused on actually seeking to implement controls that will provide the best protection possible for the information assets of the organisation employing them.

Another key challenge continues to be the issue of finding information security 'buried' in IT, when the clue is in the 'information' bit, rather than the 'security' bit, as it were. The realm of information security cuts across all aspects of the organisation and its operations, therefore you need to have a degree of influence and oversight across all elements of operations that rely on information sources in order to deliver and progress. What, in reality, does that leave out?

Make friends and influence people

By now, most organisations should already have information security best practices implemented to some degree in the organisation. However, there are still many who have it buried in IT in such a way that the struggle to implement the necessary safeguards is an ongoing one, and new projects are set up to try and achieve compliance with external legislation, regulations, standards, contracts or government-led requirements that must be adhered to. In order to be truly effective, these initiatives require constant explanation as to why you need to be linked into various activities and other change-related projects that you may stumble upon along the way.

The ISM role also requires a level of listening. At this stage, in so many organisations, there have been many, many change programmes. This can lead to fatigue being experienced, so people can tend to be resistant to any further attempts at delivering on change programmes. Therefore, the best way to ease the forward momentum required is often to allow people a short period of time to get those issues that they feel are blocking progress at the present time off their chests. Early scheduling of introductory meetings helps to get this listening phase out of the way. The ISM cannot afford to be either a wallflower or a shrinking violet! You need to be out there, amongst the people, as it were! Once you have heard the issues you can usually implement solutions that you already had in mind, as the concerns are usually not difficult to address; or, indeed, you can frequently point out to people that there are already controls and safeguards in place that may not have been adequately explained thus far, but that are likely to be appropriate for providing protection.

You have to show a certain level of commitment to delivering on the change in order for people to start to buy into the idea that things are going to be different. The ISM has to be seen to realise some quick wins as early as possible in the life cycle of the intended change programme. Actually, the ISM has to be seen to live and breathe security in all that they do, day in and day out: always wearing their employee (or equivalent) badge; always encrypting their data; always backing it up, etc. If you consider all the controls we ask our users to bear in mind on a daily basis, the ISM really must be seen to be doing them, and doing them well and with ease in order to prove that security need not be a hindrance and to evidence that it has both value and meaning. You also need to have almost a superpower of awareness – we will continue to delve into this in the forthcoming chapters.

Given how much 'transformation' everyone has been going through for more than a decade now, it is always helpful to ensure that you have adequate background information on the organisation and its cultural make-up and challenges, including what's worked before and what hasn't in the realm of change management. You will need help in galvanising the resources, communicating the changes, etc., including from those folks in human resources, training, corporate communications, etc. You've got to make links and friends across the entire organisation, way beyond the expected IT/ICT restrictions.

In larger organisations there are usually people responsible for the issuance of corporate policy, who also need to be positively engaged. If this is not the case, some level of governance review of policy must occur at your information security management forum (ISMF) meetings, which you should schedule on a regular basis. All updated documentation should be required to have some level of management sign-off prior to release into the operational environment.

Writing policy in isolation from people will render it doomed to failure, so it is vital that this work is done in conjunction with key stakeholders. You need a wide portfolio of support across the organisation. With any element of security change to your secure infrastructure amendments to policies, procedures or controls are usually required, and it is vital that these changes are made in order for them to be embedded into the fabric of the organisation and accepted as things that are connected to the disciplinary process. There need to be obvious and active consequences for failures to adhere to policy. The ISM cannot administer this, as that is tantamount to marking your own homework. This is why, in particular, you need to have engagement with colleagues in human resources. They need to understand the requirement to ensure that employees have job responsibilities identified for information security and that these are measurable within their annual personal development plans (or whatever your equivalent is). This may also require the input of colleagues from training to ensure that relevant learning objectives are measured by individuals and updated annually.

An interesting source of assistance is the ICT help/service desk – or whatever it is called in your organisation. Get the management of this area on side early, understand how many people are normally operating it, and establish what their level of understanding is with regard to information security issues. Is it, for example, that they get increased calls for password resets after significant holiday periods (Christmas, summer, etc.)? What other key issues are they constantly receiving queries on? You need to identify these key elements and frame them in language that explains that they are part and parcel of delivering good information security for your organisation. This will enable the help desk staff to see where you are coming from (your paradigm), and hopefully to better understand if your change agenda ultimately involves increased help-desk calls as a result of confused users not quite understanding the message you are pushing. This is so often the case, usually in spite of the hours you have spent painstakingly explaining the changes to their managers, and to them, through e-mail notifications, newsletters and intranet bulletins, etc. – i.e. doing all that you can! You can further help the help desk by providing them with cheat sheets and FAQs to make sure that they have the right answers to hand for each phase of your security change programme. This will help both their understanding and the level of service they are giving to the user population – a win-win all round.

Befriend the installations team, too. Depending on your organisational set-up, you may have the luxury of still having one based internally; otherwise, it may be an outsourced function. Either way, it is valuable to get to know the teams who are actually going out to your various office locations and having interaction with your users. They should be able to provide some level of interesting feedback with regard to how your infrastructure is being used 'in the wild', looked after (or not), treated, handled, managed, etc. They may have many war stories they can recount that will provide you with a wealth of information regarding the reality of your user base in terms of their level of PC literacy, and such knowledge can pay dividends when it comes to key changes you may wish to implement further down the line.

Make friends with the database administrators (DBAs) too. They hold great insights into the systems that they guard with regard to user behaviour, incidents and experiences. Equally, the DBAs will need to be kept abreast of back-up and recovery strategies and requirements, and will need to ensure that they have documented their activities and best practice with regard to system management for the systems for which they are responsible. Such input and resources will be invaluable to the ISM.

You need to make sure you are closely aligned with the other compliance functions in the organisation: data protection, freedom of information, risk, ethics, legal, records management and information governance. These may be separate or combined functional resources. If you are lucky, you will have some responsibility in all these areas. While this can sound daunting, it is ultimately where the profession is heading, as oversight of all the elements of information asset protection provides the best chance of ensuring you can provide the required amount of information assurance for all involved.

External providers may also be important to the delivery of a successful infrastructure security change programme, e.g. kit providers, and recycling and destruction providers. We will return to the latter, in particular, in *Chapter 3*.

The corporate communications team is a really important strand in all this. If you are lucky, it will be large enough to have marketing and communications people amongst its number on a permanent basis and will be well used to structuring messages (both good and bad) and understanding the kind of tone and delivery that suits your organisation. You are going to be expecting a change in behaviour from all your users (or at least that's what you should be aiming for) and, thus, you need to engage with them from a number of vantage points – i.e. what's worked in the past, what hasn't and, thus, what might work in the future as part of your communications roll-out. You need a theme, a strap line, a motto, an avatar, etc. All these elements can make your programme of activity appear more real, tangible and visible across the organisation. The users need to feel that they are part of something. Belonging is a core human need in Maslow's Hierarchy (the middle layer) and is no less important for us security people to be aware of.

There's always a need for a 'list' (well, if it's good enough for Santa Claus!)

There are some key fundamentals that you also need to have as 'stock-in-trade' information to hand, and this list grows over time, the more interaction you have with your organisation. Here are some examples.

How many users are there?

You may find that you need to get to the bottom of why there are so many potential systems with a list of employees in them. The staff directory that you find through an intranet may have different records to what Outlook® appears to hold. What you need, at least in one instance, is one version of the truth for the user population that needs to be managed in terms of policy, standards and controls, and information asset handling, which leads to your next data set requirement.

How many assets require protection in your organisation?

So often, information asset protection is utterly misunderstood and considered far too narrowly. It is one thing to have a configuration management database (CMDB) – an ITIL® element that is supposed to contain all the components of an information system. But the focus may only be either corporate PC assets or corporate IT systems, and they are rarely as up to date as they could be; it depends on how centralised or otherwise your procurement processes may be. However, there are many spreadsheets being operated locally that need to be taken into account. There are USB sticks that need to be included; there are mobile devices that need to be considered; and there are all the laptops and their contents. The task is actually enormous, in fairness. The reality is that a CMDB may not always contain the full picture. Over and above the actual hardware assets are software assets. You need to have visibility of software licensing in terms of numbers and renewal status, for legal and regulatory compliance reasons. Then you need to cross-reference this with other record sets, including your RM system or equivalent (if you have one), in order to capture the information assets that need to be protected and to start to appreciate the level of sensitivity of those information assets.

Another niggle arises when it transpires that some of the service areas/departments/teams no longer exist, so the configuration database fields containing this information will be out of date. If you are using that as part of your selection criteria for delivering system updates, upgrades and so on, it will mean some machines are neglected.

Part of asset management is, obviously, disposal. However, this is an area that can be very uncoordinated across the organisation and so it must be within the ISM's vision to join together the various strands of requirements and provide a more holistic view of the life of an asset throughout its life cycle.

For example, mobile devices (PDAs, phones, etc.) and laptops (notebooks, netbooks, etc.) may get reallocated from one user to another within a department locally. However, the IT department that initially released the configured item and noted it on the CMDB might not be notified. So the organisation may potentially end up with inadvertently exposed information assets by not following an appropriate data-wiping procedure as part of the transfer of assets process – probably because it never occurred to them that there would need to be any kind of process! This is why there are still instances of laptops and mobile phones being sold on e-Bay and the recipient finding organisational data still on there. Not only is it embarrassing, but it is a breach of the UK Data Protection Act and, therefore, counts as illegal behaviour by the data controller – the owner of the asset containing information that needed to be protected throughout its life cycle.

Another risk that manifests itself in this space is that, given the opportunity to replace your 'estate', your users can be very creative in making claims as to how many assets they have or need to have available to them. Old PCs have an interesting habit of ending up reactivated! The users may not realise that this can create licensing issues and poor performance from old machines that have not been appropriately updated and maintained along the pathway of regular IT management. But rest assured that teams have a capacity for stashing old equipment in their cupboards when they don't know what the appropriate disposal process is (or choose not to pay attention), so they don't tell ICT and the CMDB ends up less accurate or up to date than it should be.

What about USB devices? These are mobile, too, don't forget! Central control on ordering and delivering USB devices would allow for visibility of their usage. However, because the devices are so small and so portable, they are often not considered for such treatment. Users, historically, have had a great deal of free will with regard to the purchase or usage of these devices across the organisation. But they, too, need to be managed throughout their life cycle, particularly when you consider the nature of information often saved on to them and passed around and their capacity to be left lying around, lost in the back seat of taxis or left in suits for dry cleaning. The list of errors in this space is endless and depressing.

The end-of-life process should also include servers. They need to be managed when they are being reassigned or repurposed, as do routers and switches. All equipment needs to be accounted for, in terms of both its identification on the asset management database and its compliance status in relation to an up-to-date operating system, software, connectivity, etc.

So the ISM has a lot to pay attention to – keep thinking about that butterfly flapping its wings.

Of the assets identified, how many servers are there?

Your organisation may refer to a 'server farm', and you need to know how large this is, how much of it is internal and how much may be outsourced and, thus, managed externally. This will become more important, the more you try and get your head and hands around specific issues relating to patch and vulnerability management. Addressing the challenges of protecting systems is an element of maintenance that should be part of business as usual (BAU) operation. Sadly, it is all too often to be the case that this is not happening, as it is not explicitly annotated as part of various individuals' full-time roles. Information security is, in so many cases, not 'baked into' the organisation, as has been described in so many articles, papers, blogs and books over the last decade. This is something that must be discovered and addressed as part of the ISM's programme of change action.

What about information assets?

Over and above identifying hardware and software, there is a need to identify information assets. This is best done by the ISM, in conjunction with the records manager and/or the information governance manager, taking a proactive stance and providing the user base with a checklist for consideration. This should cover:

- how the information is stored;
- what volume of data constitutes the information assets;
- how legislative requirements are met (data protection, freedom of information, retention periods, etc.);
- who it is shared it with;

- whether these colleagues are inside or outside the organisation;
- how many people there are;
- on what devices the information is stored;
- what kind of impact there would be if there was a loss of the information assets.

What version (or versions) of antivirus is (are) running and how often is it (are they) being updated?

Again, there may be many questions that could be asked in this area, but you need to know the basics to get you started. There are still IT people out there, in organisations that should know better, who believe that Linux, Unix and platforms other than Windows® do not require antivirus updates. No computing environment is immune.

How many systems administrators are there?

You need to be aware of this, so that you know the size of one of your key audiences. Then you need to know across how many platforms, corporate systems, etc. those system administrators (sysadmins) are stretched. You need to know how many people have administrator access to how many different systems – and you don't always have to accept the reasons for this! Nor should you accept that there may still be passwords that are unchanged from default or are particularly obvious. You also need to be able to log each user to the IP address of the PC that the user registered at – access control management needs to happen across a number of layers of the open systems interconnection (OSI) model stack.

1: August - Pulling a team together

There are reasons why issues like this keep featuring in the 'top 20 critical' lists of security controls that need to be implemented to achieve a baseline of best practice in terms of security management across your organisation.

It is also worth gauging how long sysadmins have worked for the organisation. Over a period of time, sysadmins can become quite personally involved with their systems, in the sense of feeling a great deal of ownership of them and responsibility for them. This may need to be tempered with a requirement to look outward enough to see and understand the increasing levels of threat over time. If ongoing education and attendance at various workshops, conferences, etc. has not been part of your sysadmins' role, then they may not be aware of the scale of system management required and the need to make swift and deep changes to configuration, sufficient to provide a greater level of protection.

How often are systems updated?

Obviously, this is meant to be the start of a much larger conversation around patch and vulnerability management. And much like antivirus updates, it's not just Windows® that needs patching. Every platform can be exploited by an attacker and, therefore, the more protected you are, the less vulnerable you will potentially be.

How many exceptions (deviations) to policy are there?

Identifying this can tell you a lot about the current organisational culture and view of information security. If there are too many exceptions being sought, either the security policies have been written too harshly or

23

impractically, or management and/or the users are not taking the requirements seriously enough and are seeking to demote the intentions by finding ways around policy requirements, rather than seeking to mitigate gaps in compliance.

All exceptions to policy need to be made on the basis that they will only be agreed to for a period of time, rather than being allowed to remain unchallenged on an ongoing basis.

When were access controls last reviewed?

Every organisation appears to have retired accounts that are still showing as active on their system, so there is always somewhere you can start to tidy things up. You need to correlate the number of users (identified employees) with the number of active accounts and manage these. System users are often not cleansed out of systems, and this won't help if you have any migration requirements. Early review of last usage and deleted users will be a helpful strand of your work.

The process of retiring old accounts still seems to suffer from a lack of timely co-ordination between management and HR, and yet it seems like such an easy issue to resolve. Somewhere along the line, it is clearly not perceived as being of enough importance to warrant the much-needed attention required to bring it up to the expected level of security control to provide true information assurance. Obviously, the more these kinds of scenario can be automated or dealt with by online forms, the better. The ISM can usually assist in smoothing the process by ensuring these kinds of suggestions are made and followed through.

Another common bad practice with regard to user access control is that of copying users' accounts, rather than creating appropriate, new role profiles, and ensuring that the new user being created on the system has a clean instance. Given the volume of ageing or non-retired accounts, this is another aspect that needs close review and ongoing management.

Then you find out that agency staff may not come through the HR route, as departments can employ people directly for part-time contract requirements. This may mean that those users are not part of the leavers' process either. There are a lot of different types of worker these days, and you need to capture the different routes through which they may join the organisation, so that their before, during and after journey of employment can be tracked and managed throughout the life cycle. Without a level of co-ordination, weaknesses arise.

What level of information security awareness is there across the organisation?

By now, most organisations have delivered some level of user information security awareness briefings to their employees at least once. The trick is to plan to do this more than once and to ensure that for every employee attending a session, an acceptable usage statement is captured that can be retained in their personnel file. The statement needs to capture whether they are considered to be a remote user or not, and this should then tie them to some assets. Background verification checks may need to be carried out for some individuals, too, and these should also be retained in personnel files. These checks should then be linked to their training profile and to confirmation that policies have been 'read and understood'.

How is incident management addressed?

You need to be able to identify:

- what an incident is;
- what its impact might be – on the organisation or on an individual to whom it might relate;
- what it looks like for different audiences;
- what people should be looking out for;
- how this can be communicated, and to whom.

As the ISM, you have a significant part to play in ensuring that the mechanisms are in place for everyone to be able to report incidents, so that these can be captured and reviewed in order to assess whether there is policy change required or behaviour change, or both. Joining up incident management across the organisation will go a long way towards addressing risk management. Incidents need to be added to performance management reporting, so that visibility is achieved across an appropriate management layer.

What about team and company communications?

'It's the little things that get you' is an oft-used phrase. When you discover that different departments are using their own banner at the bottom of their e-mails, some of which are referring to the e-mail scanner used and some are not, your task as the ISM has to be to attempt to bring some order and structure to the situation, with appropriate reasoning for needing to do so. As I said before, the ISM has to live and breathe security in all its manifestations, so integrity of information and output is one of the cornerstones and this is a manifestation of it operating in error. As a starting point, the e-mail system should be applying banners, so individuals should not feel the need to create their own. However, in the absence of automation, a standard piece of text should be provided that is applicable across the organisation.

A key pick-up from this small example of an ISM-related task is that consistency of delivery is what drives security home for the users. When they understand why it is that a change is required, and how, in particular, it could be applied to their own personal environment, this makes it more meaningful. Security through obscurity can be a valuable approach for achieving defence in depth – the less you display about the products you use and the versions you are up to, the less an attacker may know about your likely vulnerabilities.

What about other projects going on in your organisation at the same time?

It is very important to be mindful of these because busy employees will be distracted and pulled in all directions with a multitude of priorities. The trick for the ISM is to show how information security is part and parcel of all that busy work, not an extra in isolation. So you need to have eyes and ears across the landscape to pick up on plans and changes, as well as connections to existing teams and projects so that you have visibility of what's coming up and can ensure that security considerations are being included from the earliest possible point.

Project management

So we've seen the importance of finding the people who have a vested interest in delivering positive change and those who are going to be helpful, for various reasons. With your immediate team, which will probably be made up of predominantly IT-based skills, you may find it necessary to explain information security 'from scratch' to them in the way that you want to see it implemented across the organisation. It really has developed beyond firewalls and antivirus software, although we obviously must also still apply these technologies. I'll come back to this under BAU in *Chapter 2*.

IT people should appreciate why it is that you are getting involved in so many elements outside their domain – because you are following the information train and know about the need to protect it.

There are many risks that can befall a programme of activity. You need to know who will authorise ongoing expenditure on your project and who will require any budget monitoring reports. Finance people certainly need visibility of the appropriate reporting on a monthly basis or your project spend may very well disappear, so start with your own activity. It is helpful to know where the spend is going and is part of the expanding profile of skills required of the ISM role.

Always check the small print – suppliers can try and pull a fast one with larger customers as they don't believe that the 'small print' is, in fact, being checked. Always check the following:

- Do the hours of work tally with the quoted costs?

- Do the people coming and going in your organisation have the authority to be there?
- Has the job they were contracted to do been done properly?

The bottom line is – don't assume anything, check everything.

There are always a number of key activities that need to have taken place prior to reaching a milestone. Now, I don't want to make this chapter a regurgitation of any kind of PRINCE2® methodology, but there are basics that get applied and then people seem to end up unaware of them or lost in terms of responsibility, accountability and participation.

So, it is important at the outset to have explained your management style and your expectations with regard to the commitment of all the participants.

Also, check people's holiday commitments! You can have the best plan in the world and it all goes Pete Tong (Cockney rhyming slang for 'wrong'!) as a result of a key player not being available at a critical time within the delivery phase. A key milestone may, thus, be missed, especially if that individual is, in fact, unaware of the critical nature of their input.

These are just a few of the key fundamentals that you need to have as 'stock-in-trade' information to hand – and that the author needed to have to hand in month one of the project, in order to progress. This list grows over time, the more interaction you have with your organisation.

A managing director brought in his iPhone with Windows®
7 and wanted it to synchronise with his work equipment.
Such was his power that, in spite of being a struggling
manufacturing company in a recession, the company had to
spend money on a new server to upgrade systems in order
to allow for his connectivity requirements.

Chapter summary

This chapter has introduced the essence of a programme of
work carried out in a real organisation some time ago,
through the mechanisms of highlighting some of the key
starting points to be considered if you find yourself in the
role of ISM – either part-time or full-time.

Imagine, if you will, that each element outlined above
occurred in real time, but is being described in an active
tense sense of work that needs to be done. One learns over
time that information security is ultimately all about risk
management.

A key lesson to learn is to try and reframe your activity as
more of a programme of change than a project, as projects
are notoriously viewed as determinedly having an end – and
security should never be seen in this light. It's more a
'never-ending story'!

The next chapter progresses the programme of activity,
providing some interesting experiences and scene setting
for the ongoing programme of change being delivered for a
particular organisation. The hope is that you, too, can see
the clear lessons and links as they may apply in your
organisation.

CHAPTER 2: SEPTEMBER - STREET TRASH

Building your house from the sky down

Bono (U2), Spring 2011

Introduction

So, now that your team is up and running, you have your reporting in place and people understand what is expected of them, you are starting to get noticed and the programme of change is under way.

You have learnt a vast amount about the organisation already – if you have all the answers to the questions asked in *Chapter 1*, that is! No doubt, there are many people surprised at how interested you are in such a wide variety of issues. This is precisely how it should be. The ISM is interested in the security of information in all its forms, in all its locations, in all its transactions across the organisation and beyond. Remember, implementing and maintaining information security is not solely about focusing on bits and bytes – it requires the triad of people, process and technology-based solutions, controls and safeguards. Part of your ISM role is being able to express the importance of the tasks you are undertaking in executive management speak – so this is the language of risk and financials, not bits and bytes. The focus needs to be both strategic and service orientated, explaining security in pragmatic terms.

In *Chapter 1*, we looked at the requirement to know how many users there are across the organisation and how to manage them throughout the life cycle. Then you learnt that you need to check for duplicates of users in the various system resources. These may have arisen as a result of data entry errors when inputting the names originally. Not every system resource may be directly linked to a central Active Directory, or equivalent, and, therefore, there are IT administrators managing a multiplicity of systems with different directories of users. These need to be synchronised, so that the users do not lose any access rights or connectivity as a result of any data migration or server infrastructure changes carried out by IT.

Incompatible software

There are still many organisations finding that they are in relationships with third-party software suppliers that provide products that apparently cannot be upgraded, as to do so would, in all likelihood, cause incompatibilities and configuration errors. This means that any security patching or upgrading, which should have been done, has not been carried out for fear of affecting the currently working system's performance. These are large software providers continuing to deliver substandard products, in terms of not having inbuilt security, to large organisations in both the public and private sectors. This is in spite of the length of time that the importance of patching and upgrading has been an industry-relevant mantra that should amount to best practice. Many available and widely used systems currently have to be made backwards-compatible by internal IT teams, rather than being patched to a future state of security. Given the number of users this can impact in some organisations, it can leave hundreds of PCs not patched to today's expected security levels. It is unacceptable to continue to tolerate or support this situation.

It seems there are people across the IT industry who do not fully understand the OSI model – the seven-stack layer (see *Table 1*). Security needs to be happening across many of these layers, all at the same time, which requires a great deal of consideration and configuration management. People selling products may not appreciate this sufficiently to understand the impact of what they are going to be leaving an organisation with. There will then be a great deal of maintenance and support required afterwards to get the product, as sold, to deliver the anticipated benefits, , and usually there is an extra cost that was not factored in. This needs to be addressed and the ISM continues to need eyes in the back of their head to watch out for potential problems from all angles!

Table 1: OSI model (source: Wikipedia Commons)

Data unit	Layer	Function	
Host layers	Data	7 Application	Network process to application
		6 Presentation	Data representation, encryption and decryption, convert machine-dependent data to machine-independent data
		5 Session	Inter-host communication, managing sessions between applications

	Segments	4 Transport	End-to-end connections, reliability and flow control
	Packet/ datagram	3 Network	Path determination and logical addressing
Media layers	Frame	2 Data link	Physical addressing
	Bit	1 Physical	Media, signal and binary transmission

In the UK public sector the austere time and recession environment have been circling overhead like a black cloud since 2010, and continue to cast a shadow even now – as a result, there is the madness of a central government approach to developing authentication systems, which is taking a great deal of time to get right despite its importance. Meanwhile, local government bodies have had to develop and implement their own, as they could not wait for the centralised system to be implemented. Yet more cost and integration issues will arise over time as the achievement of standardisation and centralisation is sought in an attempt to reduce overheads. In the meantime, the duplication of effort in terms of software, technology and policy requirements is significant, and the users are ultimately part of the fallout as they end up having to manage a number of authentication devices to access different systems and conflicting set-ups. I have often had to suggest to users that they will need a Lara Croft-style lock-and-load belt in order to contain their various authentication dongles, USB devices, mobile phones, PDAs and access cards.

This is, of course, almost the antithesis of achieving good security as the users will psychologically want to keep all their kit and equipment together in one safe place; but, in doing so, they may expose themselves to a greater degree of threat than the organisation is comfortable with, in terms of managing the risk. In your day job, as ISM, you will have to solve many of these conundrums, which require constant reassurance and 'fleet-of-foot' responses to questions and queries from the user base – and often slightly different answers for management.

Remote workers

Another conundrum within this space is identifying and clarifying who is a remote- or home-worker. You need to know:

- Are all remote users remote?
- Are all home-workers working from home?

Your 'remote-working policy' or equivalent really needs to contain appropriate definitions of mobile workers, in as many scenarios as possible, in order to ensure that the set-up they are using is the most appropriate one (safe, secure and reliable) and the one that can be best supported.

Possible ways of categorising the different types of roles are provided in *Table 2*. The original source of this helpful approach was a white paper written by Siemens Enterprise Communications on contact centres.

The examples provided in *Table 3* are for public-sector-type roles and organisations, but can be easily tailored to your requirements.

Table 2: Role categorisation

Profile	Description	Typical requirements
Internal		
Office-based worker	Staff who spend 90%+ of their time in the office (e.g. clerical staff).	A dedicated desk, fully equipped with ICT equipment and services.
Flexible office-based worker	Staff who spend 90% of their time in an organisation's office (e.g. managers, ICT staff).	A dedicated desk, probably equipped with a laptop and a docking station/touchdown area within each office, enabling them full access to ICT services.
Home-based worker	Staff who spend all, or a significant proportion of their time, working from home (e.g. part-time contact-centre agents).	A dedicated work environment at home with access (typically via broadband) to the ICT services they require; plus a docking station/touchdown area within one or more offices.
Nomadic worker	Staff who have no fixed work location, are often in transit, but may visit organisation offices and may also work from home (e.g. social workers).	Ability to access ICT services as/when/wherever required, including external locations while in transit, at home or in the office.

Associates		
Members	Elected members. In general, highly mobile across the organisation and external locations. High level of communication. Frequent meetings.	Ability to access certain ICT services as/when/ wherever required. Needs to manage contact. Increased use of conferencing to save on travel/meeting time.
Citizens	Local citizens who require information and services from the organisation.	An increasing number of citizens prefer to use the Internet or other media for accessing corporate services or communicating with the organisation. This could extend to ISP-type services.
Partners	District/unitary organisations, other public bodies (e.g. health, fire) and external service providers/private bodies.	Shared services and enhanced communication.

Table 3: Examples of public sector roles

User group	Profile	Requirements
Social workers	Nomadic	Spend most of their time visiting the homes of adults/children to deliver social care services. As people-orientated staff, they are often non-technical, so flexible working solutions need to be user-friendly and tailored to their specific needs. As lone workers in a vulnerable position, they need to maintain a high level of contact with support staff and management.
School advisers	Nomadic	Spend most of their time visiting schools. They also visit their main office and work from home. They have a shared PA who allocates their jobs and provides them with a link back to the organisation. In general, they have a good understanding of technology. For instance, some school advisers use Skype phones on their home PCs to communicate and collaborate with colleagues during the evening. Also, as they are promoting the organisation's technology and services to schools, they need to be seen as advanced users themselves.
ICT support staff	Flexible office-based/nomadic	ICT support staff would probably be categorised as flexible, office-based users. However, as an increased number of organisation staff will be remote from an

		organisation office, the profile and individual needs of ICT staff will also change. ICT staff clearly need the greatest levels of access to network-based systems (administrator rights) from anywhere on the network, including remote access connectivity (i.e. via the Internet).
Managers (selected areas)	Flexible office-based	Managers generally spend a significant proportion of time in meetings. These often necessitate them travelling to other offices within the same building/campus or different locations. Maintaining contact while in transit and during meetings (i.e. for selected contacts) is important. Tools to reduce travelling or wasted time, and manage meetings more efficiently/effectively, are regarded as very desirable.

Note: some office-based and flexible office-based staff may be required (or wish) to work from home/elsewhere, so appropriate provisions still need to be made. These may or may not extend to full ICT service access. The whole premise is one of flexibility in delivery.

The reason for spending some time on this, and providing resources, is that the question of who is captured under what category keeps coming up in meetings and discussions. Therefore, your best bet is to make sure that you have a clear remote (home/mobile) working policy that addresses this, so that you can keep referring to it as the central source of guiding principles to which you will adhere when you structure solutions to suit the needs of these roving users. We will be returning to this in *Chapter 4.*

Consumerisation will make this an even more important task, as you will need to have identified, specifically, what type of technology each of these users is operating in order to carry out their roles. You also need to clarify whether the devices are their own or whether they belong to the organisation, as there are clear impacts with regard to protecting the information, keeping the devices up to date and operating safely and securely.

Another aspect to this is that the increasing drive for achieving mobile and remote working for employees, to reduce organisational infrastructure overheads, may be exposing the organisation to greater risks in maintaining compliance with various regulatory, legislative and standards-based requirements. For example, if you had a number of payment card industry (PCI) users operating from home on an organisationally secured laptop, but taking credit card details over the telephone, potentially writing them down, faxing or e-mailing them, would you be happy or not? The reality is that there should be a display screen equipment (DSE) related health and safety check going on in every home or remote environment where your user may be operating. However, it is appreciated that this is a potentially significant undertaking and, at present, in most cases there is only lip service being paid to knowledge and visibility of the circumstances in which your potentially classified information assets are being handled while not within your immediate scope of control.

User acceptance testing

User acceptance testing is vital and needs to be built into all change processes. Getting the right users at the right time in your programme plan can be a challenge. Going back to your *Chapter 1* answer set, you need to know what users have access to which systems and try to create some kind of 'uber' set of users – a control group, if you will – that represents the most likely and most used combinations of software and applications across the organisation. This is so you can call on them to test your newly configured desktop or laptop build, if you are rolling out new platforms or upgrading existing ones. Again, while this may appear to be a very IT-focused task, all roads so often lead back to a perception that any issue is fault of security; as a result it really is better to be involved and fully cognisant of what is going on than be the last to know. For too long, security has had a bad rap, being seen more as an inhibitor than an enabler, and so the more that can be done to improve this perception, the better the overall information protection results will be.

Business as usual

There are many tasks explicitly described as security related that by now need to be appreciated as being part of BAU for ICT (IT). In other words, they are not solely in the remit of the ISM or administrator. These include:

- access control
- antivirus/malware
- back-up
- business continuity
- disaster recovery

- incident management
- patch management
- vulnerability assessments

These need to be explained to your IT team, so that there is an understanding of ownership and responsibility for tasks. (I am assuming you do not necessarily have the luxury of many teams of people who will be addressing each element individually. It is very much appreciated that, in all likelihood, there are fewer people doing more tasks these days)

In brief, for each area:

- Access control – IT needs to manage the process of setting up new users, deleting old ones or changing role profiles.
- Antivirus/malware – IT needs to ensure that there are up-to-date signatures and fully managed and licensed products on all nodes of the network – servers, desktops, laptops, etc.
- Back-up – IT needs to ensure that back-ups are taking place and that restores are tested on a regular basis.
- Business continuity – IT needs to ensure that it has a plan itself, just as every other organisational department needs to have a plan.
- Disaster recovery (DR) – IT needs to make sure that it has fully engaged all sections or departments of the organisation in the exercise of carrying out business impact analysis on the systems, so that there is clarity of expectations with regard to incident management.
- Incident management – IT is a great starting point for capturing incidents that are occurring across the infrastructure and the users. The ISM should work closely with IT staff to identify and categorise incidents

in order to investigate them and learn lessons for improvement.

- Patch management – IT needs to ensure that it is applying patches in a timely manner across the whole infrastructure in order to maintain risk reduction.
- Vulnerability assessments – IT needs to ensure that it is carrying out assessments on the infrastructure in order to maintain an awareness of the level of threat and to mitigate it accordingly.

The role of the ISM is to set up the framework – the policies, procedures and guidelines – and to create and deliver security awareness sessions to communicate and explain all these. Thereafter, everyone else has to actually do their part, continually, not just immediately after the first rush of enthusiasm following the launch of the framework. This is an ongoing task, and not a project with an ending, hence the earlier references to a programme focus, rather than a project focus, being more appropriate.

Information ownership

In a great many organisations, there is a large divide between IT security and roles that address information governance topics, including data protection, freedom of information and RM. Given that the focus of an ISM is that of protecting information assets and enabling business initiatives with security enhancements and implementation, and that of an information governance manager is knowing when, within the bounds of legislative and regulatory requirements, to share, disclose, save, store or publish information, if the two are not working hand in glove there will be trouble: this way madness lies! It is vital to have a close working relationship. In an ideal world, the aim should be for a coalescence of the roles (teams, if you are very lucky), and this will actually provide the organisation with the best overall approach to protecting its information assets, keeping them safe, secure and reliable over time. We'll return to this in *Chapter 9*.

Physical security

The longer you are in an organisation, the more physical security starts to take shape as a really valuable mechanism for providing visual aids, which you can use to as examples of the change that people need to embrace. Every day, you should be able to identify an event that has happened or find example of an event that is likely to happen, just by doing a tour of your buildings. The following is a real (true) story.

Incident

At 09:45 am, I observed the 'facilities' personnel bringing a trolley cart between two buildings to collect confidential waste bags and remove these for shredding. The trolley was left unattended as the single operative went into one building, up and down many flights of stairs, to collect bags on each floor. As the trolley got stacked up, it was left for longer and longer. It was still unattended at 11:25 am, and by 12:35 pm it had been removed, but had obviously become so stacked that a bag dropped off and the operative didn't notice, so it was just left on the street (see picture in *Figure 1*). As a sad reflection of these unsafe and uncertain times we live in, the mentality now is that you wouldn't pick it up in case it had a bomb in it. But, as I had observed the chain of events, I felt on safe enough ground and, ultimately, found the contents to be extremely disappointing – nothing juicy or newsworthy! So actually, in reality, the bag need never have existed at all as the paper materials therein could have been recycled a long time previously or shredded on site.

Figure 1: Confidential waste

Top tip – *always* have a camera facility available to you! I'm old school, so I carry a proper camera in my handbag at all times (where allowed) while on sites. Obviously, most mobile devices have photographic capability these days, so this is not hard to achieve either way. You are then able to capture, visually, the 'wrong' behaviour that you are seeing so that you can 'play' it back to your user population to explain what it is that you want to see done differently.

By using the example and photograph in the above incident while delivering user information security awareness briefings, it made it all the more real for everyone as the location was so close to a regional newspaper that anyone else could have taken the bag straight there instead; irrespective of how dull the contents were, the story would have been in the data breach itself.

Side issues were raised as a result of talking about this one small incident to a wide audience. For example, other locations had to wait too long for their collection of confidential waste, which meant that there were often times when quite a considerable collection of bags could be found. This is the equivalent of the jars of sweets in a candy store – slips like this are tempting and present an opportunist thief with a target. Then there are the constant examples of keys left in cabinets, doors left open that shouldn't be, etc. We will return to this later on.

Other physical security issues transpired during the month, which really started to highlight the need for broadening the scope of coverage and understanding. It is often the case that facilities management deals with physical security and there is little communication with ICT, or wherever information security is housed in the organisation. Since 2011, there has been a lot of discussion around the need for convergence of these two key functions, in an attempt to address these gaps. Having spent many years implementing ISO27001 ISMSs, however, I couldn't see the need for such convergence as it implied that people had not been doing ISO27001 properly, given that physical security is an embedded and expected requirement. It is important, either way, to watch out for exits and entrances and put yourself in the mind of a would-be criminal. Consider how you might gain access to your building and, in so doing, what you can see and what you could walk out with. It doesn't have to hold obvious value at the time, but may have a sell-on value that you have not currently considered.

It is extremely important to live and breathe security visibly and physically, as well as electronically and technically, so that your user population sees it in action and believes that it is being taken seriously all the time.

Password management

Here is another tale from the trenches.

A key piece of the project implementation was to change from user-defined passwords to a Windows®-driven password management process that demanded a minimum eight-character alphanumeric password. The decision was to apply a global setting on the Active Directory, as anything else required phased changes that involved a lot more effort and management for both users and ICT staff.

This required communication across several areas:

- ICT help desk – to ensure that they were ready (in terms of staffing and knowledge) for an increase in call volumes on the day of the password change.
- ICT systems teams – to ensure that all system administrators and database administrators were ready to change the passwords on the systems for which they were responsible and, more particularly, to ensure that the systems themselves could handle the new password requirements. This turned out not to be the case in all circumstances, which led to a need for a high volume of password policy exceptions in the short term, something you want to avoid if at all possible, and the need for a great deal of system remediation in the medium to long term.
- Personnel – in order to ensure that the changes to user behaviour in no way contravened any rights and obligations issues. It was also necessary to capture any issues relating to long-term absence as a result of sickness or career breaks, as those individuals would not be around for all the information about the password change and then would return to their PCs, probably having forgotten their passwords, and the reset would require more interaction.
- Communications team – in order to ensure a phased set of messaging was delivered in various organisational briefings – online newsletters, posters, etc. Management briefings ensured that cascade messaging could be provided in face-to-face team meetings. Organisational briefings were done at the following intervals:
  - o 100 days
  - o 50 days
  - o 30 days (one month)
  - o one week
  - o the day before

> • Third-party providers – this was an interesting group to have to factor in. The more we try, from an ICT point of view, to standardise and consolidate our infrastructure and make the user experience more holistic and joined up, the more providers themselves continue to be frustrating to deal with as a result of differences in operating platforms and system development. In this case, the mobile device (PDAs, etc.) providers, in particular, had to be embraced as part of the process as there were two competing technologies in play. It was not possible, in either case, to easily apply the password policy change across all the users who had device identities in the system, as their devices would lock up and get confused, creating gateway buffer overflows due to the number of false messages being sent requesting password resets. 'Expect the unexpected' is a pretty helpful ISM mantra to have!

The whole implementation of the above seemed to have a new challenge every day, over the first week of its implementation. There were server password reset traumas – servers that had not been rebooted in years needed to be safely downed and then restored and, when doing so, there were often no skills available to deal with the technologies faced. Unknown passwords on systems for which the original developer was no longer employed meant that resetting these was pretty much impossible.

The same was true for legacy applications that needed to be kept running, but no other maintenance could take place as nothing could be changed if you could not log on to the server. Integrated applications had complications, too, and PCs that had to be 'always on' needed to be identified. So they were forced, at least once, to reset to the new password configuration, so that as many configuration items as possible were in compliance with the new password policy rolled out across the infrastructure.

The ISM's task is usually to implement the sleekest, most polished form of policy suite for all circumstances, which simply may not always be possible. There are many scenarios you cannot have imagined in advance when you are writing policy documentation in isolation of the real business of the organisation. So there is real value in wide communication during the life cycle of the policy suite – from the formulation stages and delivery through to the implementation stages.

Laptop management

Why do users have laptops that they never connect to the network? Laptop users need to be reminded to connect their equipment to the network when important updates are occurring in order to be appropriately maintained. No excuses! If a user is not prepared to do this, then they should not be provided with the equipment. This kind of requirement must be embedded as part of their contract of employment and job working conditions. Laptops should be connected for updating purposes on a specified regular basis and, if this does not occur, there must be some mechanism of recourse and recall in place, so that the users can see that policy is enforced and, thus, the rules have meaning and are adhered to.

You also have to ask yourself the question 'why do some people have laptops at all?' What do you do when you know that there is a laptop that has been plugged in as new two weeks ago, but it has a monitor plugged into it 'because the resolution is better', and a keyboard and a mouse? Why not have a PC? There are some people who will always have a desk and office-based role. Even though, in most procurement processes, it is apparently 'easier and quicker' to purchase a new laptop, this really needs to be resolved in order to ensure that an appropriate desktop is provided that is attached to the network in the right way. Otherwise, it leaves the user with the difficulty of having to find a safe place to store their laptop every evening – or worse still, having to take it outside the organisation (presenting risk in itself) when there is really no need.

The lesson learnt so far is that however large or small your organisation is, and no matter how available technological solutions for inventory management are, there seem to be ongoing challenges with identifying all configuration items, managing them and protecting them appropriately. Again, this is unacceptable and we really must be doing better. The ISM needs to be taking on much more of an 'enforcer' role to ensure that people do not lose focus on the tasks in hand, however manifold they may appear.

Chapter summary

This chapter has reviewed a number of key chunks of activity that the ISM should be spearheading in their organisation, depending on the level of maturity of the ISMS in place.

In reality, in order to ensure that the asset base of the organisation is at an appropriately secure level, significant investment is often required to continue to roll out security-based change requirements. Part of the challenge for the ISM is to develop the right communication channels across the organisation, in order to best leverage existing resources to deliver the desired end result.

CHAPTER 3: OCTOBER - COMPLIANCE MAY BE ONLY SKIN DEEP

Introduction

The experience that is behind the writing of this book is that of usually swooping in at the last minute, with about six weeks to deliver a compliance state for an organisation. However, most organisations tend to realise very quickly that saying you've done it (security) doesn't necessarily mean that you are it (secure). The capacity to successfully fill in forms and 'get through' audits is staggering, when you consider the gap between the contents of the verbiage and the reality of the infrastructure and operation across many organisations. It may be that 'compliance is only skin deep' and you have to actually dig below the rhetoric, then formulate a plan to achieve the stated claims of compliance and ensure that the level of required security is embedded across the organisation.

The 'business' is always seeking to understand what the return on investment will be for any security-related spend. Cost-benefit analysis in the security arena is notoriously tricky, and often fruitless. Some would see us as being 'ambulance chasers' – we are constantly coming along after an incident has occurred (a breach, a loss, etc.), being asked to fix things after they have gone wrong, swooping in to solve the oversights of others. Or, we could be seen as being fundamentally insurance salespeople, advising that a particular approach (policy) is taken that would reduce risk and protect the organisation in the event of an incident arising, while not being clear on the level of likelihood, even though the impact may, indeed, be very tangible.

There has been a sufficient volume of data breaches and incidents of loss in the last few years to provide a plethora of real examples to share with your organisation, with the stance of 'there, but for the grace of whoever you worship, goes us'. In other words, if we don't implement the following security-related controls and safeguards, this could happen to us, and we wouldn't want that, would we?

Information security policy

A key cornerstone of the work of the ISM is building an appropriate information security policy suite of documentation. The first big hurdle is to ensure that the intended audience understands that a 'security policy' is, in fact, not a single document in itself, but a suite of related policies, procedures and guidance that gets built up over a period of time, and is reviewed and added to constantly. It is an ongoing task, as maintaining records and documentation is always hard work and so is rarely afforded the continual attention necessary to be meaningful.

As a career ISP, invest in books on this particular subject. There are many good ones out there, some of which have been mentioned in the reference section at the end of this book. One good resource in particular is Thomas Peltier. He describes the 'tiers of policy' and places the key information security policy as a Tier 1 policy that applies to the whole organisation. Tier 2 policies exist underneath this, addressing specific subject-related matters (personnel security, business continuity, access control, etc.). Tier 3 policies are considered to be application or system specific. The larger your organisation, the more documentation you can see needs to be built up to create your ISMS. This requires a significant overhead in terms of maintenance to ensure that the guidance you are providing for the organisation is followed; it needs to be in order to maintain the security of the information assets that are being created, stored, processed, entrusted to everyone and shared widely.

Policy creation needs to be risk assessed, as do any requested, planned or intended changes to existing policies. There may be impacts on users, business processes or technologies, and these need to be captured, addressed and understood by all parties. Different teams need to be engaged, depending on the scope of the policy (procedure or guidance) to form either a change control or a governance review level, so that you are not left writing your documentation suite alone in a vacuum.

The outputs have to live and breathe, and be used by everyone in order to evidence compliance. Otherwise, there will constantly be references in audits to policy not being adhered to, and this will give the appearance of insecurity when, in reality, it may be that the policy was written wrongly and needs to be changed to meet the working practices of the organisation more appropriately.

One way of forcing the agenda is to ensure that employees sign off on the information security policies most directly applicable to them. For example, they should certainly be signing off in terms of 'I have read and understood …' on electronic communications usage (e-mail, blogging, social networking, instant messaging, etc.) and remote/home/mobile working. This should be tied in with their personnel file and, if possible, ensure that all employees are provided with a personal information security plan for each year, which will include merit for attending annual awareness briefings, adherence to policy, application of password changes, etc. You should be able to see that this can then be linked to your requirements for metrics and measurements, so that you can start to evidence the effectiveness of the whole security policy piece to senior management. You are obviously aiming for a near 100% coverage of all full-time employees, plus some level of coverage for ad hoc workers.

From your point of view, as ISM, you need to have input from legal, personnel, facilities management, IT, etc. – depending on the circumstances and intentions of the policy documentation itself – at both the creation and the review stages, prior to release and implementation. This means having a planned programme of delivery of documentation across a timeline that may have to be agreed with these parties and a line item on the agenda of the ISMF, or equivalent, that reviews the latest documents ready for revision, approval or issue.

Policy documents themselves need to be short and punchy, direct and to the point. They are a clear statement of the stance an organisation is taking on a particular technology, people or process issue. They should be supported by procedural documents, or controls or standards. Organisations have different terminology for their chosen structure of documentation and, wherever possible, you need to resonate with this, so that your work is seen to be in keeping with the 'house style'. Security policy documentation should not be hidden away in the IT department.

As a note of caution, be wary of 'death by policy'. It is easy to fall into the trap of creating one for each and every situation (or assuming one should be written), rather than ensuring that there is a higher-level, all-encompassing policy that is technology agnostic and supported by appropriate procedural documents, control standards or good practice guides. There are those who use a perceived lack of policy ownership as a way of halting progress, i.e. waiting for responsibility to be decided. If you are bound by an incessant need to follow protocol, it may be that this will hamper momentum. Hence, there is a need for brevity in the writing of the documentation and the written word should be enforced as quickly as possible.

Managing corporate antivirus

The average computer user knows that they should have an antivirus program – and they even know that they should update it regularly, even if they don't actually do it! So there is certainly no excuse for an organisation that supports a large number of users not to be doing something effective in this space. However, there are many different products on the market and, because of the complexity of system designs (back to the OSI stack, I'm afraid), it is possible that conflicts could arise between the chosen corporate antivirus program and a departmental application. Experience of this can render your systems exposed as it may be that, rather than progress with a planned update to a new more secure version of a corporate antivirus, you have to 'roll back' to an older and, by implication, less secure version in order to maintain the functioning of existing corporate applications. This is usually as a result of conflicts that are already understood by the third parties who are supplying the corporate applications that are suffering from this conflict. As I have said before, we should not have to put up with this in the IT industry, but it seems to be part of some kind of unspoken set-up that is maintained, but that is ultimately costing us all dearly and is rendering our information assets ill-protected.

Greater complexity has not brought greater security, that's for sure. This is clearly not a new issue - Bruce Schneier, security guru of note, wrote about this in 2007 (*see www.wired.com/politics/security/commentary/securitymatte rs/2007/05/securitymatters_0503*) and again in 2008 (*see www.schneier.com/blog/archives/2008/03/security_produc _1.html*).

Standard build and image

The implementation of a standard build of machine is an IT strategy deployed in order to ensure that all desktops, laptops, etc. are managed across the infrastructure in a holistic manner (having been purchased through one procurement agreement from one provider) and in adherence with all the required security-related policies. Rolling out a new 'image' on that 'standard build' may be needed – simply replacing the machines would no doubt be the easiest option, but this approach may not be possible because of a lack of financial resources available to you.

Depending on the size of your estate this can obviously take a great deal of time to achieve for all machines, so you need to work out a process. Deploying upgraded software across the network would be the most sensible approach, i.e. using a technological solution, rather than a people-based solution (one where you would need to visit each machine), but there are many organisations that still have a long way to go in terms of gaining efficiencies from the deployment of technologically appropriate solutions.

In spite of your best laid plans, because of the vagaries of different systems, the standard build approach may not work on every single machine, for every single instance, as the combination of different applications can cause conflicts in system operation. So, having spent time developing the 'image' you want to use for all desktops to be rolled out, what do you do when it has issues? In the case of the real situation in the background of this book, we found that macro settings in certain corporate systems caused problems with image roll-out; more because, in fact, once one user has a bad experience, it can taint the new standard build for many others. Part of the difficulty can be that, while the intended conflicting system may be on a replacement programme, there may be a time lag between the implementation of the new, non-conflicting system and the present day and, thus, your users have to remain frustrated by system glitches.

You need to be able to manage the communication very carefully and ensure that you resolve any niggles very quickly. The implementation of a new 'image' across your machines may be required in order to roll out security-based enhancements, but it will quickly be used as the excuse for slowing the project whenever something goes wrong. Any negativity needs to be nipped in the bud swiftly, so that future security enhancements are not hampered by any lingering memories of poor performance caused by bad press.

Microsoft® Baseline Security Analyser (MBSA) proved to be a very valuable tool in the arsenal of available technologies to help identify the security state of assets. MBSA is a software tool released by Microsoft to determine security states by assessing missing security updates and less-secure security settings within Microsoft®

Windows® and Windows® components, such as Internet Explorer, SQL server and Microsoft® Server macro settings. As we were finding macro settings' issues with corporate applications, this was a good place to start. Knowing the volume of machines that needs to be kept up to date is a starting point (we mentioned this in *Chapter 1* as being one of those key questions that needed answering). Having a view of the spread of their security status is extremely valuable. Your resources may be stretched too thinly to be able to achieve full compliance with all policy requirements in one delivery, so to be able to prioritise machines against their security status makes the task all the easier and you can justify your approach on the basis of the evidence you have gathered.

Software licensing has to be managed in this process, too. This is also a key issue when rolling out new images. You need to know the current status of the number of licences for each application and what the requirements are in each team, section, department, directorate, etc. – not just from an operational point of view, but obviously from a legal point of view, too. Compliance with all requirements and knowledge of the maintenance level, length of licence and number of users, concurrent or otherwise, are all information elements required for managing the software assets in your estate.

Password management (again)

In *Chapter 2*, we focused quite a bit on password management, but, as with all elements of information security management, they are ongoing and repeat regularly. With the roll-out of the password change segment of the security change programme, it was necessary to deal with various devices and users, and manage both the human and the technological responses to the change. In order to achieve this, support was required to ensure that centralised control of the estate (mobile or otherwise) was possible, so that equipment could be recalled. This was important in order to ensure that upgrades were applied, so that users were not able to avoid responding to communications requesting product returns.

As part of the communication process it was necessary to visit various teams, departments and directorates, and deliver briefings to the management and both their regular meetings and the update sessions that were carried out as part of their monthly activities. Getting information security on to the agenda as often as possible is hugely valuable, so that people can hear what your plans are and what is forthcoming in the programme of change. More importantly, it is an opportunity to listen to the employees and hear what their concerns are; you might learn, for example, that they are still writing down their passwords(!) or that they don't have enough lockable cabinets - but I'll come back to that one later in the book.

Consumerisation

Consumerisation has been building as an industry theme during recent years, but I have certainly been dealing directly with it since at least 2009. Users have wanted to have all the capabilities and facilities of their own mobile devices for quite some time. However, they lack the appreciation of how this might affect the organisation from a legal standpoint. For example, in some instances using their own devices (BYOD) would involve breaking motoring laws – you are not supposed to be operating a mobile device while driving.

As an organisation you usually have a wide range of obligations that must be seen to be adhered to, and these are supposed to be documented. Even if you are not following a framework like ISO27001 you need to know the legislative landscape within which you are operating and to be able to explain to your user population that their home experience may well be different (faster, etc.) than their work experience of technology, but that this is necessary in order to manage an infrastructure often operating across a wide area network and a vast number of individuals.

Third-party management

There are a number of layers to third-party management. You may have many third-party software suppliers providing a spread of products to your organisation. Depending on the nature of these, not all of them will be directly security related, and there are still many providers of IT within the industry who are well behind the understanding curve when it comes to information security. So, the role of the ISM is to be the educator in these circumstances; to be aware of the contract terms and conditions, the intentions of the purchase and the expectations of the delivery, all within the bounds of protecting the information assets that the system is ultimately designed to support, process, store, share, transmit, etc.

So when we found we had a third party e-mailing zip files with patches for their products, which were being quarantined as unrecognised files, it led to a couple of different responses. As a public sector supplier, the query had to be whether e-mailing security updates in the clear (unencrypted) was the most appropriate approach. They should have known better and been providing a more secure support service. It presents a negative image of security when government-related providers still have a tendency to 'talk the talk' but not 'walk the walk' in all cases.

Audit log management

Audit logs are rarely reviewed – why is this? Who looks at these and who should look at these? How often? What's the value?

The perception is that the volume of data being generated may simply be too great to actually analyse with any degree of value. However, in some cases, system owners do not know whether they are being maintained or whether anything of value is being generated. This has to be another area for the ISM to get their teeth into.

There are many levels of audit log to be tracked and some level of prioritisation is probably worthwhile. Start with the systems that contain the most sensitive information assets and seek to provide the best protection for them first. Thereafter, target those systems that have logs that provide management with data that helps focus resources – system log ins, failed attempts, intrusion prevention systems (IPSs), intrusion detection systems (IDSs), firewalls, routers and switches. There is a wealth of data to be gathered and analysed in order to get a true picture of your day-to-day levels of vulnerability and needs for patch management, updating and maintenance.

Vulnerability management

Managing the running of vulnerability scans is a vital part of any ongoing ISM role and it is alarming to read vulnerability reports from external providers where the results are so often the same:

- SANS top 10 or top 20 vulnerabilities identified (therefore, known vulnerabilities are not being addressed with known solutions).
- Defence in depth helps, but needs to be maintained – there is still a problem if firewalls and reverse proxy units functioning as expected, but those managing them are not feeling supported internally. There is not always time to ensure the firewalls and reverse proxy units are maintained appropriately – both technically and also in terms of the skill sets required of those responsible for managing the machines. This is an important point for an ISM to be aware of in order to help influence either budget spend or resource planning for future training needs analysis, as these areas relate to those in system admin positions for security-related tools and technologies.

We will return to this issue in *Chapter 6*.

Cloud computing

There is a problem that arises as you become part of a wider connected network: if any part of your own internal infrastructure, or remote locations and users, are not following the necessary security protocols and controls that you have sought to implement in order to secure information assets appropriately, then it may be that you, yourself, are considered to be a vulnerability. Such architecture vulnerabilities need to be identified on an ongoing basis, with plans in place to rectify, modify, deter, react and protect the information assets in your care.

Such Cloud implications are now more fully understood, and the ramifications of the constant and persistent interconnectedness we are all facing will continue to, work themselves out over time. We can but hope that it is not at the expense of users, citizens or their personal data, although the first signs of impact were seen in 2014 with events like the loss of celebrities' personal information from the iCloud. Ultimately, the Cloud is still hardware in a data centre somewhere – there is *still* a physical element to the technological landscape and it *still* requires securing, end-to-end. In fact, the Cloud requires far greater investment in and maintenance of security than traditional IT, so it is hard to see how the financial savings model actually stacks up.

Project management

When it comes to managing a large infrastructure-related project, where a great deal of investment is required due to consistent lack of spend over an extended period of years, plural, the ISM is often faced with a constant need to justify the requirements. This is, in itself, distracting from the day job of actually making the required changes. Frankly, playing politics in an organisation can be utterly tedious. However, there are times when it is a necessary evil that must be embraced! Too often, the cry goes up that 'IT doesn't understand the business', and you, as the ISM, don't want to be tarred with this same brush.

If you lack management support or understanding, taking the battle outside your immediate arena may be required. You need to find the right audiences and language to achieve the hoped-for aims. Always provide options, and in many ways, seek to embed the one you want in amongst options that you know your audience will never approve! Make sure that you learn what works in terms of management speak, too.

Benchmarking against other peers is helpful in order to provide management with reassurance as to your actions. Become a member of any regional groups, so that you can discuss issues, threats, vulnerabilities, experiences, risks, etc. with your peers. This helps to keep you up to date, informed and able to converse with certainty in terms of expectation amongst industry counterparts.

Security awareness theme

Each month, consider focusing on a subject suitable for the time of the year and harnessing your information security endeavours to that. It helps to keep the subject at the forefront of everyone's considerations and ensures that you are baking information security into your organisational cake, embedding it into best practice and slowly, but surely, changing the culture for the better.

Always use whatever news stories have appeared during the month. There is no shortage of these, day in and day out, that should be crossing your desk as the ISM - but they may not even register for the average user. In fact, there are many stories that appear in the news that involve information security but are not deliberately presented in this light by the media. But you can find the security element – be it a personnel issue, a physical security issue, a technical security issue or an information-specific security issue. Let your creative juices flow!

This month's information security theme could pick up on the fact that October ends with Halloween, a holiday celebrated around the world. Given the volume of malware, spyware and spooky tales to tell in the world of security, there's enough to hang your ISM hat on, if you are creative enough!

Chapter summary

This chapter dealt with a number of standard subject areas that will be part of the ISM activities on a day-to-day basis. It also introduced the idea of creating security awareness themes for each month, so that you are making the subject live and breathe throughout the organisation on a monthly and changing basis to ensure that the messaging does not get stale.

CHAPTER 4: NOVEMBER - HOW REMOTE IS REMOTE?

Introduction

There are times in your career as an ISM when you really have to put your hand up and say, 'hold on a moment', and ask yourself where sanity and sense have gone!

We can all too easily make things far too complicated. The answers we are seeking are often so simple that they are not what we first consider; nor are they easy to believe because of their simplicity.

Location, location, location

If you set yourself up with a particular network segmentation approach, it may label a significant amount of users as 'remote', and this will mean needing to apply two-factor authentication to them all as part of best-practice security management controls. Managing every user outside your core location as a 'remote user' is a significant overhead and should be avoided wherever possible. Incorporate all users into the whole network view, so that all users are treated as 'one', without the need for the added overheads of managing the distribution of key fobs. This will reduce their enablement, management and replacement, and prevent headaches for all users.

You need to know your entire organisational landscape, so that you can literally map it out in a meaningful way in terms of sensitivity of data, number of users, types of asset in use, software in use and hardware requirements. There are a lot of considerations per location. However, each separate building location that forms a part of your infrastructure needs to be considered as 'a node' on your network rather than a 'remote' location. They are not 'remote', given that you know where they are. They are static buildings and you can apply a level of control to the configuration items contained therein, including the number of ports being managed from each location. You need to get past any hint of 'them and us' when it comes to how IT set up their connections since, of course, you are really all part of the same organisation unless, by way of legal statute, there is a clear separation of entities.

Working with external third parties is where the real difficulties are found, particularly if there is a need for third parties to work within your own locations. Most of the challenges can be addressed through the crafting and signing of appropriate third-party access agreements or data-sharing protocols, or both. By now, there are many great examples available, so there is no shortage of resources to help in resolving these conundrums. But there will be a need to engage more widely with the likes of the legal folk, facilities management, etc. to get the best solution for all concerned.

Innovation, innovation, innovation

You may often find that there are pockets of great, innovative work going on in your organisation and it is important to find this out. If you radiate openness and positivity, people will involve you more and ensure that you are kept in the various loops. In the project, it turned out that there was an extremely interesting and ground-breaking public sector piece of work going on that had security challenges. Because I had been out and about, banging the security drum positively, those involved felt reassured that they could engage with the project office and get the support they needed in order to ensure that their own project was a success, too. Their biggest challenges were with third parties and addressing remote-working challenges, as identified above, and most of the issues were resolved through careful crafting of the necessary agreements.

For the ISM, the difficulty is usually that such projects will have started without involvement from ICT, due to long-standing expectations or earlier frustrations related to either a lack of knowledge or lack of support. By not engaging positively the innovative project, which will happen anyway because such is the way of things, will be running risks that the project team is not be aware of, because they have none of the necessary skill sets amongst them to consider the data- and information-based risks.

Information labelling

ISO27001 has long suggested that information handling should be approached through the classification of your information assets. In the UK public sector, there are various labelling options (also known as markings) available for information assets and these require particular handling at each level. For example, sensitive personal data, as defined in the Data Protection Act 1998 (DPA) is the equivalent of *restricted* data in government speak and needs to be handled in a particular manner. In the US, this is often referred to as personally identifiable information (PII) and a broader net of definitions is cast to include more elements, so you need to know which is the most applicable to your organisation in its entirety.

This is a notoriously difficult element of the provision of appropriate information security and requires a great deal of thought and consideration. Deciding to apply protective markings to information means that you need to have the option of doing so in all systems, through the use of templates in your chosen 'office' product suite for example, and you must also be able to apply the labelling through the e-mail suite. What about messaging sent through instant mechanisms and through mobile devices? These areas all need to be considered from both a technological and an operational (practical) angle. Will the users really apply the labelling on each and every occasion? Can technology be applied that will help to ensure that they do? The answer to the latter is yes, but, of course, it comes at a price.

Lessons learnt

Maintaining a lessons-learnt log (LLL) as you go along through your change programme is a very valuable exercise. Ensuring that you write it up and present it is even more useful, so that it can be shared with others and so a wider audience appreciates what can be learnt from experience. This is a normal part of good project management and a security improvement programme can certainly benefit from the exercise.

Table 4 is an edited version of an LLL that should resonate, given how much of it has strands of common sense running through it!

Table 4: Lessons-learnt log

Issue area	Description	Commentary
Start earlier	The organisation compressed efforts into activities dictated by their 'what can we get away with' mentality, with a two-month window, and did the 'minimum' to gain connection to a secure network infrastructure. This left ICT workers overstretched, stressed and behind on their normal day jobs. It left users bewildered by the scale of change to their desktop/working environment and frustrated by the number of niggles that needed to be ironed out through the process of change. A number of the niggles were as a result of mistakes made by the overworked ICT project team members, compounded by a rudderless systems team and servers that had suffered appalling neglect over an extensive period of time (plural years).	If a project looks too difficult to do, it probably is – but fear is not a good enough reason to put off starting the processing of action sooner. Invariably, there will be resources available to provide the appropriate advice as to how best to tackle the 'whole elephant', and they need to be engaged sooner and relied on more heavily initially for skills transfer. Bottom line: start earlier and provide more management support for the project team. Ensure knowledge is gained in the subject area early enough to appreciate the scale of the task.
Working together – including	Once the team were galvanised, and empowered sufficiently	In reality, most projects are really not isolated activities and

bringing the 'customer' in early on the project. But not engaging everyone!	that they felt their contribution was both valued and welcomed, their activity level increased significantly and had a hugely positive impact on the ultimate success of the project. Bringing the customer in on the project early was hugely beneficial.	so there is always a need to engage across all team members and keep people informed, even if they are not on a specific project team. Also, provide the project team with a feeling of engagement, which means they have something that binds them together. (OK, so ours was partly inspired with sweets, but it helped!)
Holiday management	Active project management requires rigorous attention to any ongoing reduction in people days available to a project, particularly during known busy periods and holiday periods (e.g. July, August and December). This has to be calculated in terms of actual number of days lost in any one week; if you are running a project in a compressed timeframe, this is unsustainable. The worst loss in one week was 32 days!	You would have thought this was blindingly obvious. However, managing single points of failure becomes an impossible task if the project manager has no influencing capabilities over the project team members' managers – or there is no active management support that recognises team members need extra time to do their security tasks properly, rather than on top of their day jobs. So set ground rules and boundaries

		in week one and make sure commitments are adhered to and priorities appreciated.
Loss of momentum	On several occasions, a loss of momentum (LoM) was experienced. This was as a result of the culture, which tended to see this entire process as an entirely separate project from BAU, even though all the snags that were stumbled upon were as a result of BAU misconfigurations. In particular, there was a LoM from a successful extension application (i.e. an external deadline extension); there was a LoM during the summer holiday period and there was a further LoM as a result of having gained the compliance approval without continuing to close down the items on the snag list.	Ensure management support is consistent and sustained.
Project funding availability	Without the injection of the executive-approved funding, this project would not have succeeded. The funding was only granted following significant effort by the externally recruited ISM, their preparation of	Ensure that those charged with the task of delivering a significant project are adequately resourced and, if not, that only those with the necessary skills are

	various business case justification documents and delivery of executive briefings and presentations.	put in front of executive management, with the ability to speak in a language that will resonate appropriately.
Understanding wider implications	Somewhere along the line, you have to understand that IT works on a 'seven-stack layer' and deep security infrastructure improvement projects usually deliver across all seven layers in order to provide the requisite level of protection for the nature of information traversing the network.	Ensure vision of impact and likely coverage is captured at the outset, and on an ongoing basis as the landscape and requirements continue to be changed and formalised.
Interpretation of requirements	This relates to the 'start earlier' lesson learnt, because actually an earlier start would have afforded the adoption of the preferred solution, which was the application of all the requirements to the whole network rather than to a segment. Either way the technical solution adopted, in conjunction with external consultant advice provided at the time, left the organisation with a lot of work to do to maintain the current compliance expected.	Ensure the right skill sets are available at the earliest opportunity. (Bit of a chicken and egg situation, this one, because if you don't know you need to know a certain skill, then you don't know, do you? Donald Rumsfeld, anyone?)

	This also relates to 'lack of technical skills' (below), as without the necessary internal skills to see the likely pitfalls, there was an element of 'the blind leading the blind'.	
Lack of documented processes	Because people didn't follow existing documented processes where they were available things were made up and guessed at. Under pressure this creates mistakes which take more time to be addressed. (*See also 'bottom-up decision making'.*) The pace and scale of change meant that actions were taken 'on the fly'.	Ensure documented procedures are available for all known BAU tasks in all areas – and where they don't exist, build them into the project as deliverables. All changes need to be raised through the change request process, so that they are appropriately tracked.
Lack of server management	Servers are not patched and kept up to date. There is no tangible ownership and day-to-day housekeeping of the server 'farm'. The state of the servers, their lack of ownership and proper management, puts the accuracy, integrity and availability of those information assets (including users' and citizens' data) at risk on a daily basis.* Lack of server	Ensure patch management is a responsibility and active role within the infrastructure management. The servers, at the end of the day, are the custodians of the crown jewels of data that the organisation has a responsibility to protect.

	management meant that servers were not up to date enough to be repurposed, so new kit had to be purchased at short notice and rolled out in a hurry, without the requisite security hardening applied; this was then (thankfully) picked up as a vulnerability that had to be addressed. So double the work was done, time and effort that could have been better spent elsewhere. This led to tasks taking longer than expected and each security control element became more laborious and more long-winded that it would otherwise have been.	
Lack of SLAs	Service level agreements (SLAs) need to be in place between service areas and ICT, and internally between teams in ICT, to support each other and provide an appropriately expected level of service in response to requests (rather than just ignoring things or 'shrugging shoulders').	Documented SLAs help everyone to have their expectations set and hopefully met (and sometimes even exceeded!)
Lack of data ownership, management and prioritisation by	ICT ends up being responsible for issues that are, in essence, not of their own making, but are the	Data cleansing is required – particularly when migrating to new systems. It is better to

users	responsibility of the users. There are also links with green IT work, because just adding another server into your farm should not be the answer every time.	cleanse than to take erroneous data with you. There are links here with file management, and training in it is required. Implementation of a proper RM file plan structure on the servers is required (it is appreciated that this is easier said than done!) Users must be encouraged to take more responsibility for the data that they are, let's face it, creating on a day-to-day basis.
Lack of role profiles	User access rights are currently not adequately managed and this needs to be addressed, so that groups of users can be migrated together in the future on the basis of their expected access rights, permissions, mappings, etc.	Less user disruption is possible if the role profile exercise has been undertaken - to identify who is doing what function, where, and what system access they require to do that job, on the basis of applying the 'need to know' principle.
Lack of service desk management	There was a need to 'pump' out messages to the users across the whole organisation, saying that	Ensure that a) the service desk is appropriately staffed

commitment	the service desk would be experiencing an increase in call volume as a result of a specific project workload and to be patient. This was difficult to achieve without the proper involvement of representation from the service desk itself.	to deal with project ebb and flow, and b) that you communicate with users en masse, so that they are aware that while they may be 'screaming' for resolution, there may, in fact, be an operational priority that exceeds their own immediate needs.
Ensure kit is ordered in a timely manner	There was a significant risk of time line slippage as a result of delays in ordering the large volume of PCs required to deliver this project – in spite of knowing that it was a requirement from the outset and knowing the supplier's lead time in advance.	Ensure orders are placed as early as possible within the project – even though it makes the figures look scary initially (i.e. lots of spend up front) – but at least you can then plan the roll-out of equipment in the sure and certain knowledge that you actually have it available to you.
Desktop 'image' problems	Systems were included on the desktop image that were not needed – and some were missed out. It is not clear who did the user acceptance testing and why this happened, given that someone on the 'customer' side signed off the image as appropriate. This is	Ensure that the service area properly signs off on user acceptance testing of whatever is intended to be implemented for them.

	symptomatic of 'bottom-up decision making' – see below.	
Lack of recognition of and reference to data protection and security issues in contracts	There were consistently issues with regard to third-party suppliers not being adequately bound by appropriate contractual arrangements that addressed privacy concerns (data protection and security).	Ensure all third-party suppliers are bound by appropriate contractual arrangements that address privacy concerns (data protection and security). Engage with procurement personnel to ensure this is addressed in contracts, as well as at a local level.
Lack of software licensing management	ICT staff and responsible information asset owners were unable to be clear about who had access to what software at their desktop (or what they should have access to).	Ensure that you have an adequate configuration management system that captures all hardware, software and information assets, so that these can be appropriately identified, managed, secured and controlled.
Windows® takes scripts literally	An intelligent ICT developer wrote a script to copy all the users in A–J only, but Windows® thought it was smarter than the programmer (!) and copied only all the files beginning with A through	Ensure time is available to understand the ramifications of the written word in script language from a development point of view – but also

	to J, rather than everything under the user beginning with A through to J. And, randomly for a user, it picked up a six-year-old email signature block and other users couldn't see their .pst files or their address books for quite some time.	ensure there is time to test system upgrades.
Embedding passwords in systems is a bad idea	Embedded passwords need to be identified as early as possible as, once you enforce a password management policy that requires a change every 90 days, a great deal of overhead is then added. Passwords have been embedded in Access® databases and also in externally provided applications.	Ensure that applications and systems across the organisation have been identified and addressed within the required password rules.
User migration issues – corrupted privileges and excessive permissions	FAF = file and folder – permissions were a huge issue in managing user migration from one area of the network to another. User moves created a mismatch in server datasets and locations, for mapping drives and shares. Corrupted privileges in the shared and home areas, as a result of the way the user migration took place,	When undertaking a large-scale system or server migration project, wherever possible encourage service areas to create a new, clean file structure for the teams and the shared area of the service – identifying who needs access to which folders. Apply new

	meant that operations staff could not resolve issues as they normally would, as they did not have the requisite rights. This was going to take some time to unravel, time that was not being allowed for within the day jobs of project team members.	permissions from the top down (cascading them across the folder structure).
Lack of technical skills	Translation of security issues across existing technical disciplines proved difficult without an IT or InfoSec officer in post dealing with ICT colleagues on a day-to-day basis. There was no knowledge transfer regarding risks, implications and impacts, and without this or allowing for these skills to develop over time, it was difficult for many ICT members to appreciate the potential scale of the challenge.	Ensure that there are those capable of horizon scanning across the ICT landscape within which you are operating – both technically and from a security point of view – so that the two end up more in synch than in competition with each other. There really is no need for divisiveness in the delivery of ICT strategy and ensuring security is baked in alongside this.
Back-up/restore issues	Problems arose when restoring .pst files. This was a technical resource issue on the servers and needed to be addressed in order to ensure that the project team could successfully migrate larger numbers of users during	Regularly test support applications available to ensure that they operate as expected. It sounds so obvious when you type that and read it cold – but in the reality of a busy ICT team, it is

	later phases of the project.	easy to see how the obvious can get missed and forgotten – so make a note!
Storage copy issues	Problems were experienced with the infrastructure in place to provide storage for users, as security issues meant that it was necessary to do manual copies and restores. Again, this added project delays and needed to be resolved prior to rolling out more widely for the intended mass user migration.	As per the previous comment, ensure that available resources operate as expected – without security conflicts – as these are exactly the kinds of issue that turn people off to security. They assume that it is going to slow up their system or cause problems, rather than solving them.
Lack of SLAs	SLAs need to be in place between service areas and ICT, and internally between teams in ICT, to support each other and provide an appropriate, expected level of service in response to requests (rather than just ignoring things or 'sloping shoulders').	Ensure documented SLAs exist as these help everyone to have their expectations set, and hopefully met (and sometimes even exceeded!)
Lack of controlled user registration and deregistration	There was a need to ensure that all users on the network were appropriately authorised to be there and were captured in terms of their systems and building access, and that this was monitored	Ensure that there is a 'new starter' form and a 'leavers' form (and a process to support these) on the intranet (or equivalent). More devices are being

	and controlled throughout their employment, right through to their eventual departure. There was also a need to put in place mechanisms for addressing long-term sickness, career breaks, etc.	added to the environment all the time (often directly by the employee) and these need to be factored into a 'leavers checklist', in particular.
Cloning live user data on test servers	Test servers were, in the main, clones of the data that was held on the live servers, wholly in contravention with industry standard best practice, the Data Protection Act and the British Standard BSI BIP0002:2003 – Guidelines for the use of personal data in system testing.	Adhere to industry standard best practice – the Data Protection Act 1998 and the British Standard BSI BIP0002:2003 – Guidelines for the use of personal data in system testing, ensuring that live data is not used in test situations.
Lack of privilege management	ICT users and generic accounts were not reviewed in order to justify their creation. This relates to the need for role profiles.	Ensure that users are provided with the access to the systems they need on a 'least privilege' and 'need to know' basis, rather than on the basis of copying the last-known easy user to hand.
Bottom-up decision making	As a result of the lack of clear senior ICT management support for the project, its mandated requirements and its basic good housekeeping	Ensure executive management understand their responsibilities with regard to the required protection of

	expectations with regard to information security management, the project team consistently had to make infrastructure decisions that should have been done through a management risk assessment process. This left everyone feeling exposed – but ultimately something had to be done. Inaction was not a sustained option. Senior information risk ownership needs to mean something.	information assets for which they have responsibility within their organisation. Ensure the role of senior information risk owner is carried out by someone who understands information risk management requirements.
Never miss the blindingly obvious!	Direct Internet access affected all Web-based systems. Making changes to firewall rule sets had significant impacts on users and consequentially on the service desk in supporting calls as a result of disquiet.	Ensure good communication is provided in a staged and phased manner in order to pre-plan events and ensure everyone is ready for the potential impact of system and infrastructure changes.
Lack of policy enforcement	This was a significant issue across many areas. In particular, as a direct result of a lack of enforcement users were able to download whatever they wanted, whenever they wanted it. This had, in some instances, brought viruses into the machines and the network and	Ensure clear policy statements are available, as well as appropriate supporting user guidance. Also ensure that metrics and measurements are in place to ensure that policies are being adhered to and user

	created maintenance and management issues in terms of supporting the desktops and laptops. Without a definitive, (rather than 'infinitive'!) software library in place to refer to, it was impossible to categorically state to a user what was and what was not acceptable in terms of software downloads.	enforcement is evident – as are the consequences of not following policy.

* While the server management issue was experienced in 2009, and was worrying enough then, in 2014 the same situation continues to exist, so the lessons are not being learned and improvements are not being made. It is depressing to report that there is little sign of the IT industry understanding the need for appropriate server management as part of ongoing environment health maturity.

Security awareness theme

This month's information security theme could pick up on the fact that November contains Bonfire Night, very quickly after Halloween. Utilising the 'Remember, remember the fifth of November' mantra, you can play on that and deliver messages around 'Remember, remember… your removable media devices!' or 'Remember, remember… to clear your desk before you leave every day!' Or take it up a notch and go for a fireworks-related theme.

Chapter summary

The lessons learnt above pull together the experiences outlined in the book so far and address many of the recurring themes. If information security is not being built into the organisation from the ground up, ensuring that it is part of the structure, it is a much harder task to make progress so it becomes a constant task for the ISM. If you are lucky, you have management who will take such lessons learnt seriously and be able to support you in providing the impetus to deliver on the changes required.

The next chapters flesh out the increasing breadth of focus that needs to be embraced in order to achieve holistic information security management.

CHAPTER 5: DECEMBER - OH, FOR THE SAKE OF YET ANOTHER PROPOSAL ...

Security improvement programme

In this particular instance, there was an initial budget to deliver a particular goal, then a realignment of expectations following the achievement of that goal. This was because in reality, what was put on the submissions that were required to be presented to external auditors was not the reality of what was actually going on inside the organisation. Not untypical. So a plan of action (in security terms, this is usually called a security improvement programme (SIP)) was put into place to address the compliance gaps. The gaps were way beyond just technological issues and spanned all three points of an imagined triangle of people, processes and technology.

By now, a couple of months down the line from the initial upgrading of compliance to an external connection requirement, the SIP was moving along apace. However, executive management required many more business proposals in order to explain why a quite significant amount of further funding was being sought to help with addressing these gaps.

In spite of the ability to continue to deliver change on an incremental basis without it having a significant impact on anyone's bottom line, senior management need constant evidence of how these improvements are making a difference and to whom. If the evidence is not compelling, it can become incumbent on the ISM to provide senior management with visually convincing reports or, worse still, you may find yourself having to write further proposals to hold on to the budget you have already secured, in order to ensure that you are allowed to continue to spend it on the security enhancements as planned.

In many ways, this approach is flawed and harks back to my opening statement – as long as 'doing security' is seen as a project, with a beginning, middle and, most importantly, a presumed end, then management find it hard to understand why there is a constant demand for further investment, resources, technology enhancements, etc. But this is the reality of the landscape within which we are operating. Our information assets are now more highly prized and more actively sought after than ever before, and so the role of the ISM needs to involve constantly educating staff and management and raising awareness, highlighting the latest trends, threats, vulnerabilities, risks and mitigation strategies.

Fax management

There are still many organisations where facsimile (fax) communications are the most reliable medium (and, in some cases, most secure). However, in order to ensure a consistent level of safety, fax handling procedures may be required as a mechanism for reminding people how to use the medium. The answers (solutions/controls) are simple once explained, i.e. there is no real rocket science involved. This is the beauty of real information security laid bare for users in a way with which they can resonate. The solutions are simple and easy to grasp.

Table 5: Faxing – what can go wrong

Issue description	Mitigation
An individual incorrectly transcribed the number to which a fax was sent, resulting in the intended recipient's sensitive personal data being sent to a personal residence. The owner of the residence notified the organisation of the incident and shredded the document (thankfully).	Recommended documentation of the disclosure for audit purposes. Instructed to ensure staff confirm the fax number before faxing sensitive personal data and follow up with a call to the recipient to ensure receipt. Update the information security messaging around usage of faxes for all staff.

Image build again

As there were a number of key deliverables contained within the change programme, one of these – the delivery of a secure image on to all desktops – continued to be a challenge. The difficulties were very often not of our own making. For example, we ended up having to take off JavaScript™ because the software from a third-party supplier was not able to work with it and it was creating conflicts with other applications. As previously mentioned, this was part of a bigger issue, as it was a well-known industry third-party supplier who had clearly not upgraded their software with patches and software updates provided by other key providers to address known vulnerabilities. So you end up having to downgrade your security to operate some of the most fundamental services using key corporate systems.

This continues to be an unacceptable industry-based situation, which the third-party providers should be embarrassed into changing – and not at the great expense of, in particular, the public purse, which they have already plundered with hefty ongoing maintenance charges for many years.

With the reality that about 300 public sector organisations using the same software, the cost for upgrading should be on the vendor and not each individual public sector organisation separately. Central government procurement – and those involved in mandating centralised delivery of systems – should be making these kinds of pleas and ensuring these changes in the future, as part of the intended savings and improvements anticipated by the UK Conservative and Liberal Democrat government coalition.

In January 2013, the National Audit Office (NAO) confirmed that the government initiatives to reduce spending on ICT were starting to gain traction. 2013 and 2014 saw a significant programme to reduce the usage of private sector organisations and consolidate suppliers, and asked all of them to reduce their costs for service provision by significant percentages throughout the period. It is feared, however, that this will come at the expense of genuine security.

The public sector must get tougher in renegotiating contracts and demand better security for its citizens, whose data they are using, sharing, transferring and processing, all day, every day, and which is being stored and housed in these flaky systems across our land.

Physical security findings

There are many aspects of physical security that need to be understood by the ISM and not just assumed to be within the control of facilities management (or whatever your equivalent is).

In many cases, you will find that not all of your sites (buildings, locations) have locked cabinets where cables are sited. So, these need to be physically visited and secured in order to maintain that outward display of 'security in action'.

Figure 2: Unlocked cable cabinets

The kind of thing shown in *Figure 2* was discovered by conducting physical security reviews of teams, sections or departments, usually at the request of their management, in the early evening, when the cleaners were around. Cleaners are usually very helpful. Part of their process may be to lock doors to all the rooms that they have keys to, but if there are no keys this is obviously impossible. Doing these physical walk-arounds, doors were frequently found open that should have been locked. This exposed other weaknesses, because they provided extra access as a result of conjoined rooms, and especially when internal doors that joined several offices together were not secured. Wherever possible, I carry out these reviews in a pair so that one person can make notes and the other can take pictures. The visual evidence is the most powerful tool you can imagine for showing users and management the error of their ways. It is the information security equivalent of holding up the mirror, so that they can see what's wrong, and by implication work out what needs to be changed in order to effect a security improvement. This is tangible and gives you instant quick wins in terms of improved information asset protection, the importance of which cannot be overstated. All the effort in the world at protecting network security – server scanning, etc. – cannot reduce the risk of someone leaving something they should not have done on their desk for someone else to see, photograph or steal.

With the availability of camera phones these days, anyone with their eye on making a 'fast buck' could easily penetrate your organisation through physical security vulnerabilities and then either sit down and have a good long read, or take photos and send them off to the local, or even national, press and make quite a splash.

If people had to value the information assets they handled on a daily basis, like they do currency, then they might end up better protected. But the items are so easy to discard that it becomes more difficult to encourage consistent protective behaviour. Information labelling and handling can help in this area – ensuring that markings are given to the information assets being used, stored, handled, shared, processed, transferred, etc.

There are a great many files that should be marked as 'restricted' and kept permanently under lock and key – and the keys need to be registered and controlled, not left out on display. But this will take a significant culture change and education effort.

So, we need to start with personal responsibility – people really need to take on board that they need to be actively participating in protecting and caring for these files. This means locking them away at night and then secreting the keys appropriately. It means keeping their rooms neat and tidy and not allowing stacks of cardboard to pile up, nor prioritising stacking newspapers over stacking files.

In the majority of cases, keys were left in most cupboards, drawers, etc. – and on one occasion it was even possible to locate the 'stash' of all the keys to all the doors in a drawer in a unit, and another stash on top of a cupboard in a corridor.

Why is it that there is always 'kit' left around? In any office you go into, rest assured you will find old equipment that is unused – perhaps a telephone or two that need to be decommissioned and a printer. There are proper recycling companies for electronic waste in operation these days that can make the task of kit removal so much easier that there is really no excuse for collecting clutter.

Consider, also, the age of the information that may be readily available. Papers are usually left lying around that are older than the 'current year'. Given that most organisations should be operating a proper RM programme with a records retention schedule in place, having documents lying around that are outside their immediate period of use is inappropriate, as these should be in the archives or destroyed. The ISM needs to work closely with their records manager – if such a role exists. If it doesn't exist then the ISM needs to take this on as part of their functionality, in order to provide the appropriate breadth of protection to information assets for their organisation.

Part of your task is to try and get into the mind of your colleagues to help you explain why you think what they are doing is wrong. I have seen some interesting prioritisations in my time – a neat stack of newspapers on a shelf inside a cupboard near a door, and yet there were files out on both the desk and the shelves (all identifying individuals). People usually claim a lack of space, and yet the picture in *Figure 3* shows just how much shelf space was available.

Figure 3: Virtually empty cupboard

Some people seem to think it is appropriate to leave their filing on the floor when they run out of space. Why would that ever be considered appropriate? Each office needs a dedicated person who does a 'sweep' every evening to watch out for these information traps.

As I say, getting into the mind-set is tricky. So, what's wrong with the picture in *Figure 4*?

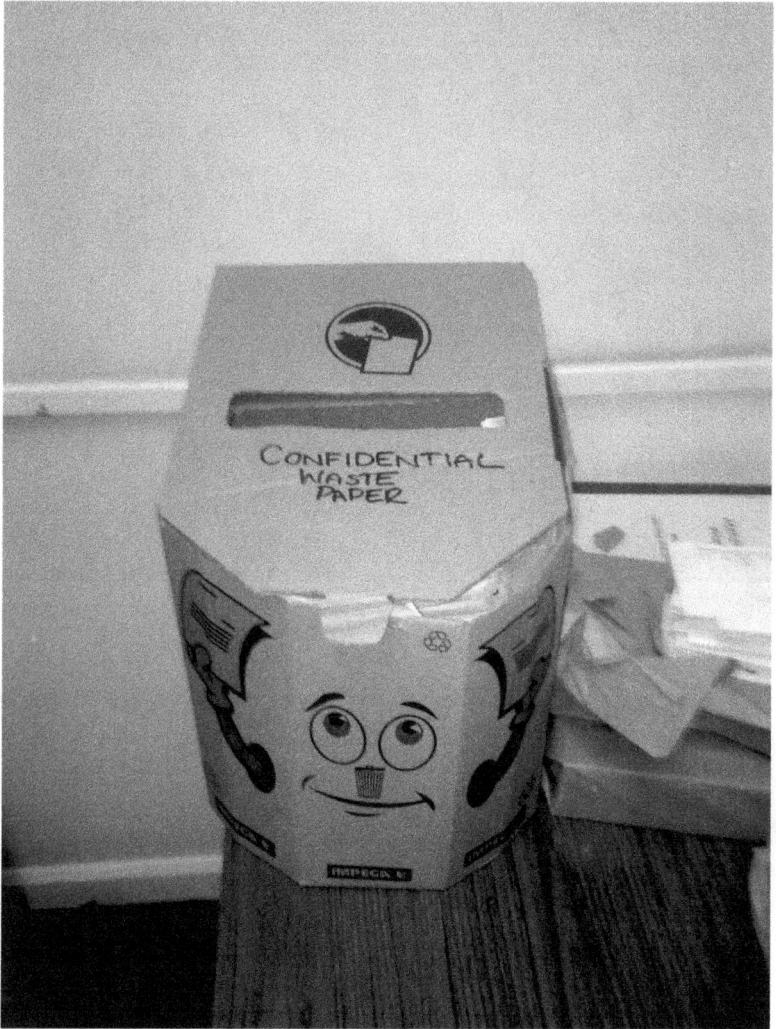

Figure 4: Confidential waste bin?

A confidential waste bin should be one that you cannot put your hand in to get papers out; it should be lockable, and the keys and access should be tightly controlled. This is like the best a kindergarten could come up with and is not what you would expect to find in a mature and professional organisation. But, until such issues are pointed out visually, the required change doesn't occur, because the attitude becomes 'it's the way we've always done it'.

In one office I visited, there was a supermarket trolley being used for file storage! We're into the second decade of the 21st century, and yet some offices still appear to be operating like something out of the 1950s. It is simply astonishing what people tolerate on a daily basis.

Expect the unexpected – there may still be floppy disks lurking in people's desk drawers. There really is no point in keeping these if you have no mechanism for reading the data. If this is the case, they need to be securely destroyed – shredded, for example.

Any build-up of waste does not look good – overflowing waste-paper bins are definitely not to be encouraged. The first question has to be 'why isn't the paper being recycled?' Then you check the contents and consider whether, in fact, it should have been placed for shredding or confidential waste. Equally, any build-up of confidential waste is of concern, especially when it is not being stored behind locked doors. Again, it makes too easy a target; someone could simply steal a bag at random, not knowing what jewels of information might be contained therein – but you never know your luck, and that's why it's called an 'opportunistic theft'.

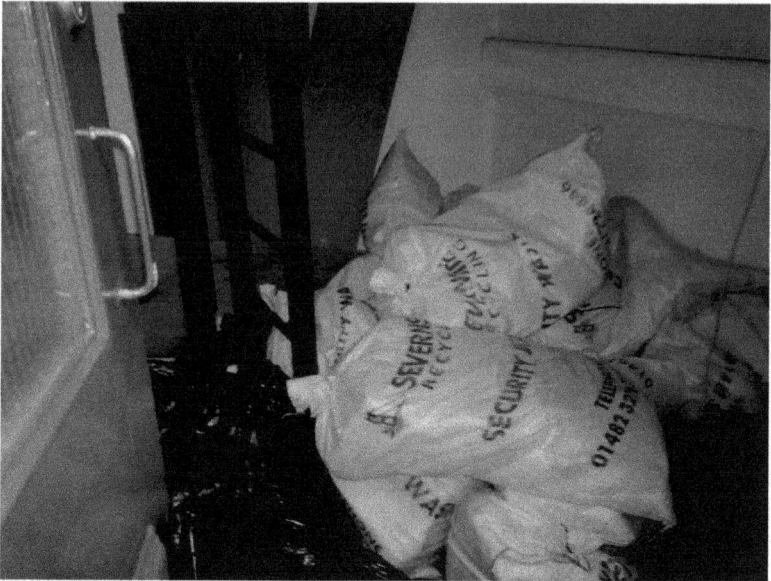

Figure 5: Awaiting collection

Physical security solution suggestions

- Wherever possible, recommend some reorganisation of office filing to make best use of the available storage. The space crisis is rarely as bad as you are led to believe, given the volume of Christmas decorations, tea bags and old (out of retention period/should be in the archives) papers you can find in cupboards!
- Seek to ensure that files in regular use are locked away as a matter of course when not in use, and ensure that no papers are left out on desks at the end of each day.
- Make it mandatory that any files that identify living individuals are locked away at the end of every day in a secure storage area.

- Move the files that are not required to the appropriate secure storage area – either external archive storage or onsite secure storage - in conjunction with your records manager, if you have one.
- Ensure rooms that need to be locked at the end of the day are locked, with the keys removed!
- Seek to increase staff awareness on the issue of information security and the importance of reporting issues to the correct person.
- Arrange for all redundant equipment (telephones, printers, chairs, desks – everything, do not be selective as it just becomes divisive) to be removed in the appropriate manner. For example, electronic equipment should be removed in compliance with the Waste Electronics and Electrical Equipment Directive. (*See http://en.wikipedia.org/wiki/Electronic_waste*.)
- Ensure that exposed cabling and power supplies are secured. This means the blindingly obvious – i.e. make sure that no one could walk up to any cabinet or similar and unplug anything just because they can, or because the mischief-maker in them thinks it might be funny to see what the end result would be. You may need to liaise with your equivalent of facilities management to put the right physical protection measures in place (lockable cabinets, cable boxing, ducting, etc.).
- As an overall physical security improvement measure, build the right kind of messaging into information security awareness briefings so that all your employees know what to be looking out for, and understand and appreciate the importance of reporting even the smallest of issues to the right person, in a timely manner.

- Ensure that you have an appropriate information security incident handling process to support this. We will discuss this in the next chapter.

Other security tasks for this month

Environmental concerns

I have already mentioned the need to be aware of as many projects as possible, so that you can ensure that security is being woven in. Most organisations are in the process of ensuring that their IT strategy meets a 'green' agenda – consolidating data centres, reducing carbon footprints and impact on the environment, etc. Some of the more useful technology to appear in this space is the kind that helps to put your desktops, etc. to sleep when not in use. For the users across your organisation, there are security implications that need to be considered with regard to leaving machines on overnight depending on what machines are used for. Messaging software is a particular risk.

Information security awareness briefings

You need to be aware of the project and be aligned with it, so that you can assist with the right kind of communication, particularly as your information security awareness briefings may be giving out the wrong message.

By now, we were four months into the security improvement plan. Briefings had been delivered to thousands of employees on a one-time basis, face to face. Work was now required in communicating with both personnel and IT training colleagues to ensure that the delivery commitment was picked up in a way that would ensure a repeat redelivery 12 months hence, with reminder notifications to all employees to undertake the supporting computer-based training (CBT) module that was available across the organisational intranet. This all needed to be made available to new starters as part of induction and a plan of delivery was required for contractors and agency staff, too. Also, for those workers who did not have access to the intranet, it was important to provide a 'train the trainer' function to ensure that local delivery of the security awareness briefings could be carried out, so that no one was left out.

The positive benefits of ensuring that the delivery had been done on a face-to-face basis, with one trainer providing a consistency of message and style, were beginning to be reaped. The users were starting to report more incidents, advising us of concerns and asking questions. This highlights gaps in policy understanding or in security infrastructure implementation that you can seek to address.

'Kit' movement

Users have become much more tech savvy in their home environment, without a doubt, although the reality is actually that users are experiencing more up-to-date equipment being available to them, with faster speeds and lower prices, but with no more training or awareness of what it is that they are handling. This increased level of technological expectation in the home environment cannot easily translate to the corporate/organisation environment, as it is unrealistic. It also does not give them licence to move or disrupt existing installations in your organisational infrastructure and this must be explained to them, then enforced and monitored.

Central management systems that provide detailed logs of activity on all desktops, laptops, servers, etc. in your network provide invaluable information once analysed, and the analysis needs to be used to inform policy reviews. You need to know if a desktop is moved or if a network cable is disconnected – for how long, by whom (if possible) and for what reason. You need to be able to explain to the users why this is important and what problems it creates at the technology end, as all they see is a cable that they can easily unplug. They don't understand the 'bits and bytes' and data being exchanged through that cable.

Laptop users... again!

Laptop users still have a tendency to save a great deal of information to the hard drive of the machine and this can only be justified if the machine itself is being encrypted at boot-up. In the UK, this is particularly important, given the strong focus of the Information Commissioner's Office on this area. It (full disk encryption) is also an expectation that is spreading more globally, too, given the scale of data breaches and information losses being experienced and their impact throughout the last few years.

New laptops are being produced all the time and some of the latest models are designed without CD/DVD drives. You need to consider this if you are buying in bulk and ensure that you order the right style of equipment to serve the needs of your users. This means their work needs, not their personal use needs, given that, of course, they should not be using the equipment for personal use, wherever possible. Certain functions in your organisation may require a CD read/write facility and you need to be able to keep track of the information being written, as the assumption is that it will be either shared or stored. In both cases, this needs to be done securely. So you need to establish whether you can enforce any kind of encryption on the transport and/or transfer of that data, and maintain some kind of register of CDs/DVDs burnt and shared, particularly if you are expecting them to be returned to the organisation. These kinds of things really arise when the policy or procedure that you have written requiring this kind of action comes into contact with the real world; it can be hard to maintain such a policy so you need to be flexible enough to review, revisit and ultimately rewrite it to meet the needs of both the users' group and the organisation. As ever, as long as you are providing the best level of protection for the sensitivity of the information assets concerned, you won't go far wrong.

Security awareness theme

This month's information security theme should definitely pick up on Christmas – focusing on the aspect of gift-giving so as not to cause any religious offence. Picking up on the well-used phrase 'A dog is for life, not just for Christmas' you could pick any element of best-practice information security and the same would apply. 'Back-up is for life, not just for Christmas' perhaps?

Chapter summary

This chapter has focused on the physical security issues that can cause you difficulties across your organisation and hopefully teased out some elements that you may not have previously considered. If you change your viewpoint, you can get an even better view of your organisation – and that will really help you to think further outside of the box!

There is a real need to have a particular mind-set if you are going to be a successful ISM, and it seems to be something you need to have innately, rather than something that can be taught... although reading books is a good place to start to build a better arsenal of capabilities for yourself!

This mind-set is difficult to teach, and may be something you're born with or not. But in order to train people possessing the mind-set, they need to search for and find security vulnerabilities – again and again and again. And this is true regardless of the domain. (Schneier, 2008, p.260)

Being a security engineer gives you a certain skillset, as does being a security architect. Perhaps even being a 'bouncer' (a physical security person) would help. You need to be able to think 'like an attacker', be it a technological one or a physical one. In property law, the terms ingress, egress and regress are used to denote the rights of an individual to enter, leave and return to a property, respectively. These terms are also used in the IT world with regard to system access. You need to consider what points of egress and ingress, in particular, could be compromised (and in what way), so that you can be prepared with some solutions. Wherever possible, apply proactive, rather than reactive, security safeguards.

In becoming an ISM, you may not have started out through any kind of standard route, but if you are of a more open and flexible mind-set you are likely to flourish. Your responses need to be relatively 'fleet of foot' in order to address the multitude of different challenges that may meet you on any given day - ranging from the sublime to the ridiculous, but most often based on people and process, not on technology.

CHAPTER 6: JANUARY - A BATTLE WON

Baking security in

So why do you need to keep on explaining what your ICT colleagues ought to be doing to support BAU functions? Constantly having to explain to internal ICT management what ICT colleagues should be doing normally is a long battle - never mind that you also have to add other extra duties for an initial period while you go through a transition to a new infrastructure or new platform.

Any large infrastructure-based project can have the unsettling ability to highlight missing work that should have been being done as part of BAU. Therefore, the difficulty is that somehow this work needs to be done post-haste – both to catch up for the time during which it has not been done, and also to attempt to provide you with some relatively up-to-date data with which to work, in order to move forward in a sensible manner.

Once a project receives its initial injection of support from management and team delivery of tasks gets it to the first milestone, there is usually an immediate slip back to the day job, and you find your resources are significantly depleted and you are once again starting from ground zero. Trying to keep your changes in place can be like running in a hamster wheel –ridiculous, given that the work should already be part of BAU and of best practice in information security management, if security had been baked into the organisation properly, in a meaningful way.

Desktop refresh versus consumerisation

When doing a desktop refresh, there will always be issues of prioritisation, pecking order and contingency requirements to be juggled. There is no doubt that the increasing march of consumerisation (bring your own device) is changing the landscape of any ICT department-based strategy for infrastructure refresh. But given the age, budget and maintenance cost of some existing organisational portfolios, there are likely to be those still with this pain to go through.

Considerations must include the age of the desktops (machines, PCs, call them what you will); those with a certain type of monitor (and costing the replacement monitors into your plans is an important element of the overall cost of the budget portion); knowing which ones need CD/DVD writing facilities; knowing which ones may be for front-line services and which ones for back office; which ones require payment functionality and which ones will be in shared areas. Who needs SD cards? There are those for whom photography is an important part of their job function and, therefore, this may be a requirement.

Will switch and router cabinets require replacing, too? If so, in what order do things need to be planned out? There is a contingent disruption factor to users when this kind of infrastructure upgrade work is going on, which requires appropriate communication planning in advance, so that preparations can be made. With the volume of laptops available to users, homeworking arrangements can be put in place to help alleviate any perceived downtime or lack of connectivity expected to corporate systems.

Incident reporting

By now, more and more people should be aware of what you are doing in your organisation. Therefore, you actually start to hear more and more war stories, skeletons appear from closets, and long-standing gripes and issues start to get aired. While you may be used as the whipping person for things that may never be resolved, you need to allow an open-door policy to exist wherever possible, as within the silt may be some gold.

To make it more official, I put in an enhanced incident reporting process in order to ensure that people knew they had a 'right of say' (which psychologically can be more important an imperative than a 'mandate to say') and, thus, a gem appeared. This was to be handled through the ICT help desk for visibility. An individual 'raised a ticket' to say that they were told that they were not allowed to buy more encrypted memory sticks. As a result of this purchasing clampdown, the users were utilising their own USB sticks at home – by implication, unencrypted and probably not antivirus protected either.

The reality was that this was only reflective of a larger project-wide situation, but a member of staff raising it as a 'ticket' incident helped to expose the need to increase appropriate organisation-wide communication and to progress the intended project much faster to incorporate a wider number of users, so that there could be a greater level of protection of information assets. The particular information being put on the 'home owner' USB sticks would, in most circumstances, be classified as 'sensitive personal data' and would be labelled (protectively marked) as 'restricted' at minimum.

Either way, you need your users to be able to report incidents, and you need there to be a record of these to collect data that can be analysed and reported to management in a meaningful way. This will all help to build up your metrics so that you can measure the effectiveness of the information security management framework that you have been seeking to implement across the organisation. Incidents that occur should be categorised and reported to senior and executive management in a way that is palatable and comprehensible for them. Some people prefer numbers (rising or falling statistics); others prefer pictures (pie graphs, bar charts, etc.). You need to understand what works best for your organisation and be able to create some kind of compliance dashboard that provides a 'confidence count' for security – i.e. is the organisation, as a result of the improvement measures you are putting in place, getting more or less secure? Is it explainable, translatable, measurable and tangible?

Information security is a very subjective delivery mechanism for your organisation and continues to require visible representation to explain the benefits. People tend to notice when it's not there. This is most notable when data breaches and information losses are being experienced, particularly if the incidents arising are making it into the media (national press or otherwise). When it is working, when information security has become embedded, i.e. baked into your organisation, it is likely that people won't really notice it day-to-day, as it should not be getting in their way.

Data-sharing protocols

The industry on whose periphery we operate loves its acronyms and its reused phraseology. So, when a colleague comes and asks you what it means to be a 'trusted source', you need to be able to construct an answer! Context is, of course, very important. But how is this identified and what makes someone 'trusted'?

The difficulty is that the context is related to trying to deliver on the promise of information sharing. It seems that each agency within the public sector is making up its own language, just as each industry in the private sector does, too. You need to watch out for this, as your role as ISM is often one of translator. Wherever possible, you need to develop relationships across the various agencies that your organisation has connections with, in order to learn their language twists so that you can translate for your own colleagues. You cannot operate in isolation and, somehow, you need to try to be one step ahead. Then there are all the conflicting initiatives that are the harbingers of change attempts. Again, you need to keep abreast of these as every politically related change has an impact on an information system that will be used to produce statistics or manage a requirement; your organisation will need to secure the data on such systems and the people managing it. There are usually far wider implications from small changes than were originally considered.

But back to the 'trusted source'. It was a crossed-wires scenario where one agency was claiming that it wouldn't trust our connectivity unless we proved certain things. Yet both agencies were in the same sector and should have been adhering to the same policies, procedures, guidance, network connectivity, connection protocols, legislation, regulations and standards. It was a clear example of the need for data-sharing protocols to be in place – and for them to be meaningful, in terms of having the right breadth of security controls to support the clauses contained therein. As an ISM, you end up needing to know about contracts and agreements. This involves having to understand legalese. It hurts, but it's worth it! Data protection clauses – think of these as information asset protection clauses – need to be better referenced in contracts from the outset – either directly or as an annex in the form of a security schedule.

You need to be able to provide a sensible response to providers when their sales teams are determined to sell you the world, but the reality may fall short. In particular, with the Cloud and virtualisation intentions moving forward apace, it really is important to know where (in the world) your information is, who is going to look after it, for how long, how you will be able to get it back and how long that would take. You can't be afraid to challenge the legal jargon and ask for what the actual facts might turn out to be, because, in breach mode, it might just be too late to find things out. Time will always be of the essence. There are times when you have to be explicit about data disclosure, data sharing, data retention and data destruction, obviously, throughout the life cycle of the data.

Over and above that, you need to have a register of protocols, so that you have visibility of who signed them on behalf of which organisations, and when they are due to be renewed. This is ultimately part of your mitigation strategy for risk reduction. The reality may be that the only time you need to know this information is if something goes wrong, but the same can be said of your car and house insurance policy details. Regulatory bodies expect an organisation to have control and visibility over its information assets and know who has access to them, where they are being transmitted to, who they are being shared with, how long they are being kept for, under what conditions, in what circumstances and on what media – USB drives, CDs, DVDs, laptops, etc. Hence the need for the early establishment of the inventory as highlighted in *Chapter 1*.

There are constant perceptions of differences in security requirements across industry sectors, agencies, government and the private and public sectors. The perspective of the ISM should really be that, whatever is at the heart of the requirement, there is always a need to protect information assets; the task is finding the best way to do so that suits all. You often need to cut through all the rhetoric and polysyllables, as the solutions are invariably tried and tested – and simple – and this can be hard for people to take, as they don't believe anything can be easy anymore! But it's too easy to make things seem complicated and that isn't what you want to be known for. You want to be seen as the 'department of yes', not the 'department of no'! You want to be seen as a solution provider.

Linking InfoSec with records management

Once you have fully grasped your role as a provider of protection for information assets and solution creator for future projects and programmes across the organisation, your custodian-style role needs to extend across the life cycle of the information assets for which you are seeking to provide the protection. If you are lucky, as previously mentioned, there will already be a records manager employed by your organisation. You should seek to work closely with them to ensure that your protection mechanisms are in keeping with legislative retention requirements, amongst other maintenance elements of records' life cycle.

Certainly with the Cloud technology take-up that is continuing apace, there are some interesting access and storage discussions required moving forward. The organisation needs to establish whether it is necessary to have all of the data available, all of the time and, if not, how best to store it in a secure way that is suitable for the likely classification of the information itself. Of course, there's the rub. If you haven't identified the information assets and applied the classification in a way that labels your information to be identified and distinguished sufficiently, then it will be difficult to know how to make distinctions between the different types of information and how best to look after it.

One aspect of this is working with various project teams in order to ensure that considerations surrounding the life cycle of the information are built into the procurement process for all systems. So often, archive facilities are not considered as part of the initial requirements for intended new systems, and yet there should be some understanding that, legally, data cannot be kept forever and, therefore, it has to be managed through stages. There must be some kind of transition plan for it – from day-to-day usage, to short-term archive and then to longer-term retention.

Also, depending on the nature of the data, the security requirements need to be dictated in order to ensure the long-term safety, as well as security, of the data. There will also need to be authentication arranged for the requirement to reinstate data or to access it outside its retention periods.

Penetration testing results

As we saw in *Chapter 3*, vulnerability management is a key task that an ISM needs to manage and monitor. Part of this is achieved by arranging for penetration tests to take place on all systems and using the reported findings to manage the resultant mitigation activities.

The following are the most consistent findings from penetration testing reports:

- No one appears to be in charge of network security as a whole. This can be a result of the fracturing of responsibilities, often due to workforce reduction, which a lot of organisations have experienced in the last five to ten years, and also is symptomatic of a focus on the functionality of systems, rather than their security. This is manifested in the appearance that no one is taking responsibility for the life-cycle maintenance and day-to-day management and upkeep of systems at a network level – through not applying updates, patches, etc. – causing real risk to both systems and ultimately data; nor does anyone appear to know about the top 10 or top 20 vulnerabilities for systems that have already been identified industry wide, and certainly nobody is applying the required solutions or designing systems from the ground up so that in future they do not contain these weaknesses.

Some of the key issues that result out of the above lack of ownership are as follows:

- Blank passwords still being used on the installation of new equipment – this is a classic, and something we all know to deal with and change, but time appears to get in the way and everyone moves on to something else and forgets to go back and make the obvious changes.

- SQL database with default and blank passwords – similar to the above issue, but at least on our project it again served to highlight the scale of the issue for management and confirm that there were system management issues at a number of layers of the 'stack' that needed to be addressed.
- Passwords easily cracked – this can be a most fascinating revelation. Of course, in my case, it was the one that caught the eye of senior management the most, particularly given the password change project we had been through as an organisation. It required careful management and communication, given that the immediate assumption could have been a failure of the password change roll-out. What it highlighted, in fact, was the need to keep communicating to users the need to create relatively complex, but memorable, passwords – an almost impossible task that was made even more difficult as a result of the layers of corporate systems that still needed to be brought up to the same level of security. Ultimately, there were too many passwords for the user to manage, and highlighting this as a result of having been able to 'crack' too many meant that more effort could be directed towards seeking solutions.
- Patch management appears to not be being managed in a timely fashion, and this dereliction exposes the architecture and infrastructure to vulnerabilities.
- Excessive number of administrator accounts found – and at the time this was a disappointing finding, given the work that had been ongoing with the password change project. However, it served as a useful highlight for why the significant number of exceptions to the new

password policy regime needed to be addressed, rather than left to languish, buried and ignored under the volume of other tasks that needed to be tackled, day-to-day, on the security front.

Penetration testing and vulnerability assessments provide valuable insights into the state of the security implementation of an organisation. These are often confused. A vulnerability assessment should be considered to be linked to risk assessment. Systems (assets, resources) are identified and a value (importance) is assigned to them. Then, the potential threats to each asset are identified. The expectation is obviously that mitigation steps are put in place as a result of presenting the findings – at least for the most valuable resources and most serious vulnerabilities. A penetration test proves the vulnerabilities that are found (it is effectively a 'proof of concept' of them), providing an impact analysis of the flaws on the underlying network, operating system, database, etc.

None of the above findings are uncommon, but they demonstrate that good security practice is not in place.

It is expected that these tests will be carried out at regular intervals throughout the year. Doing so can involve some trepidation, but remember our mantra – there's no such thing as 100% security and you will never be 100% risk free, so never expect a clean bill of health. Always use these opportunities for learning and set expectations accordingly. Then plan in the remediation work alongside the, no doubt, already intended network (and other) improvements.

Here is a small further note on this, to reflect that it will come up again and again. You should consider the issue of service packs versus critical patches, as affected by the nature of the system you are rolling out, or already have available to you through your IT provision – how do you make the decision as to the order in which these should be done and on what priority basis, when your landscape spans thousands of machines? There is a difference in how the network responds to the updates and how IT deals with machines that are struggling. Where possible, you want to have these updates running in the middle of the night – harder, obviously, if you are operating in an 'always on' environment. So, again it may be that you want to cluster your machines as per our physical layout example, and be able to deploy updates to specific sets on the basis of their priority and criticality to the organisation. Whichever way you choose to do it, be prepared to have to deal with fallout from even just one machine not working 'the morning after', as it can create a ripple effect, a chain reaction of bad press across a team that extends outwards, and that's the last thing you want when you are on a programme of change – or at any time really.

Back to physical security issues

I have often wondered at the separations and silos we have built up in our organisations and our industries, and what useful purpose they really serve, apart from maintaining empires and egos. For the sake of the organisation in the future, co-ordination and collaboration are usually required. One of these fractures is between emergency planning and the need to ensure that business continuity plans are in place. It's hard enough sorting out DR plans, but these need to relate to systems. Furthermore, the business continuity plans need to relate to the business processes that utilise those systems. There is plenty of separate literature available on all this. The point made in the introduction is to get back to thinking about emergency planning in a certain way – all too often similar activities with shared risks are seen as very different. I visited an emergency planning room once and was surprised to see all of the emergency plans for each service area, with the folder titles visible (for ease of access). It was suggested, perhaps, that these could be moved into the new lockable cabinet that was available within the room, given that on a Thursday, Friday and Saturday night there were external third parties who occupied the room, carrying out night marshal activities, to whom these plans should not be so readily available. This had not occurred to the information custodians up to that point. Also, updates to the plans appeared to be difficult to manage, but they also contained a lot of personal data with home phone numbers and general contact details. So, the learning point of the visit of the ISM was that greater care needed to be afforded to this kind of material on a day-to-day basis.

Another finding was that there were two users who found it necessary, as a perceived result of previous poor corporate system performance and server storage space, to utilise 8 GB external USB sticks as their file storage system. These were stored securely on site at the end of every day. The USB sticks contained personal data including stored sickness records, timesheets, etc., all of which was stored manually as well. This highlighted a significant amount of duplication in terms of both electronic and manual data, creating storage challenges. The ISM was able to reassure the users that there had been significant improvements in the corporate network and infrastructure, and to suggest that they should review their processes, particularly given the availability of the secure storage area within the storage area network. Also, the users needed to consider that the information was not 'theirs' as such, but belonged to the organisation, and, therefore, the files needed to be more readily accessible by other colleagues across the organisation.

Beyond the emergency planning visit, there was a visit to the CCTV team which was equally educational. In general, recordings were normally kept on tape for 31 days and then overwritten. However, CCTV evidence was burnt to CDs when requested and these were kept in A4 folders in sleeves on the shelves, openly accessible, rather than in lockable cabinets. There were two A4 folders a month of collated ongoing and transferred sheets. This seemed to be a significant undertaking, and while not directly referencing people, the CD contents presumably provided visual recognition of individuals. As this represented personal data, under the UK Data Protection Act it should have been stored safely and securely at all times.

'Maintaining situational awareness' is a phrase I've heard often during the past few years. It means what you think it does – having eyes in the back of your head and being aware of your surroundings and the situations you find yourself in. With awareness, you then have to work with whatever resources you have to hand. In the case of this review, there was an extra storeroom, near a main entrance, that was literally piled high with tapes that were waiting to go to the police for appropriate shredding. The team had asked for this to be done, but it was a classic example of having asked for support, but getting nowhere. The people being asked did not appreciate the nature of the material (its effective labelling and, therefore, the requirement to handle it in a certain way) nor the potential impact if the information had ended up in the wrong hands; i.e. the request itself was not risk assessed so was sadly ignored. The ISM needed to step in and *make* something happen. These kinds of situations must not be left, but must be attended to – this urgency needed to be transmitted back to the service desk, so that they learnt to appreciate the nature of the random requests they might receive and sped up their response mechanisms to a more appropriate level.

Reduce, reuse, recycle

The programme of desktop refresh continued to rumble on as it spread more widely across the organisation. By now, there was a stockpile of returned machines that could potentially be reallocated and this required some careful consideration as to the needs of the users – as opposed to their wants and desires!

There was obviously going to be a large amount of equipment requiring destruction, having established those that were no longer of use. After all, you wouldn't want your organisation ending up on a BBC documentary. Earlier project plans included building a relationship with a recycling provider that would certify the quantity of equipment that was taken away and ensure that it was appropriately destroyed or recycled, each and every time. The physical certificates for the quantities removed were maintained as records. This led to an interesting set of statistics which could be presented to management, including the tonnage of equipment removed, the volume of that which it was possible to reuse, the volume recycled, any value brought back into the organisation, the number of machines replaced and the number of machines upgraded – all of which could be measured against the total estate to assess progress and provide useful feedback to the wider organisation.

For some machines, it was possible to provide the short-term fix of updating or upgrading the memory chips to extend their current life. More critical, machines were replaced. Some machines and connectivity were so old that they were connecting through dial-up modems. They still exist out there, believe it or not!

The project team working on the desktop refresh were trying to keep certain types of machine in single locations – i.e. all Dells in one, all HP in another, etc. – in order to ensure a level of ease of maintenance on sites. If an engineer turned up at one building, they would know what type of machine they would be facing throughout and the likely issues it would have, and would be able to resolve these faster than if there were a number of different machine types that would have complicated varieties of conflicts, system faults and failures. This, equally, made it easier to apply patches and updates across the network to blocks of machines at a time, rather than necessarily to the whole estate in one move. The more you can control the delivery of changes, the easier it is to manage any glitches that arise along the way.

On top of this, there is likely to be a quantity of old pieces of equipment out there, languishing in cupboards, storage areas and old filing cabinets across your geographical outreach, and you need to actively encourage people to hunt these out and feel that they can turn them in, with impunity – ensuring that they are appropriately disposed of or recirculated in line with your infrastructure strategy.

As a final note on this area, it is helpful to encourage people to bring in their old PCs from home, to be either refurbished or recycled in an appropriately secure and environmentally friendly way. At first reading, this sounds like an expensive (or mad!) undertaking, but it will pay dividends in the long run. You have to consider that it is likely that many of your users have actually used their own home machines to do your organisational work, reviewing reports, editing them, forwarding them on... There may be all sorts of information, sensitive, personal or otherwise, stored on that home PC, over many years of service. Taking control of the disposal of equipment is a risk reduction mechanism, appropriate in the current working environment where the Information Commissioner is expecting you to have both visibility and knowledge of the whereabouts of all of your organisational information assets, at all times throughout their life cycle.

Other security tasks for this month

Job descriptions

In *Chapter 1*, I mentioned that you needed to provide a framework to effectively manage employees before, during and after their time with your organisation. Part of this activity is ensuring that security roles and responsibilities are allocated and tasks are referenced on job descriptions. It is also worth considering implementing a personal information security plan to be linked with their annual personal development plans. This would be a plan of skills, training and development that they would commit to undertaking to improve their understanding or their performance on behalf of the organisation and ensure that they are doing all they can to protect the information assets in their care. It stems from getting the users – all users, from the CEO down – to understand that they are the ones creating the information assets that need to be managed, stored, transmitted, shared, and kept safe. ICT is only ever a custodian of the information – it is not the owner. So the user population needs to understand the importance of its role - ensuring it is tied to their annual performance and appraisal tends to focus the mind. It is even better if it can be linked to the actual financial element of it!

Users' understanding

Remember that while we assume that our users must know a lot about technology these days, because it is all around us, what they in fact know is their consumer-related experience of it rather than any level of 'under-the-bonnet', hands-on experience. So over the years many users have been sat in front of a computer and told to get on with it, with little or no training provided for them. They have had to muddle along and, if they have come unstuck, prevail upon their colleagues for assistance. But you can see the flaw in that kind of approach. If their colleagues have had the same training pattern – i.e. none! – they have a very loose grasp on the benefits of the systems they are sat in front of. It can be surprising to learn what they genuinely don't know! So another string to the ISM bow is being able to provide a safe environment - for example, an information security awareness briefing - in which those attending know that they can share their concerns and their limitations in the hope that you can help to provide them with a route through to a solution.

There are lots of users that do not know what a .pst file is, nor how to look for it. (Just in case, it's what Microsoft calls your *post* file for all your *mail*). In many cases, they never even thought to ask. They only ever appreciate the significance of this information once they lose their mail – and are grateful for learning it, both at work and to help them in being better home users, too. So it is worth explaining a bit more to them up front – the benefits will become clear as time goes by.

People management

If you are on a long programme of change, you need to be able to continue to motivate your colleagues when they return from holiday or absence, so that they continue to do a job that, by now, may appear boring. For example, the tasks may be across a significant number of machines for upgrade, replacement, repair and restore; or a large server farm that needs a lot of tender loving care on the patching side. There are a great many tedious tasks in the 'engine room', that's an apt metaphor, as these systems really are the engine that keeps the rest of the organisation motoring. You need all your colleagues – both technical and otherwise – to appreciate these bare facts and step up their game accordingly.

Security awareness theme

This month's information security theme could pick up on the fact that January is usually a time for New Year's resolutions. For example, 'So what's yours ...? Ours is to always update our antivirus ...' or 'New Year, new attitude ... let's lock down those devices!' However trite these may seem, the user population will have some appreciation for the mix of irony and humour, and at least will see that there is a theme and a messaging effort going on.

Chapter summary

This chapter really started to share the breadth of the scope of activities that can be expected of an ISM in any given month, not all of which are technologically based – nor should they be expected to be. The clue is in the title!

The next few chapters embed this broad-brush view of the ISM role with a myriad of tasks that all need to be undertaken. They also reinforce that you must understand what the purpose and intent of your organisation in its totality is, so that you can provide better advice for the safe and secure use of its information assets and resources.

CHAPTER 7: FEBRUARY - MONEY DOESN'T BUY HAPPINESS

Divide and conquer?

As an ISM, you can see by now that you have to consider yourself to be some kind of plate spinner – with a number of different sub-projects going on at any one time. This may have been done to serve the needs of management, rather than for anything designed by you. So the end result could be that nobody knows what's going on!

However, there is always a concern that your large project is like an elephant that cannot be eaten all at once. Therefore, breaking it down into a number of sub-projects is a good tactic as this will focus each team on specific tasks, rather than spreading them too thinly across the project. We were encouraged to break it down into the following:

- Port control/removable media –data loss prevention technology, also referred to as robust endpoint security, was installed at the ports in order to ensure greater visibility of the devices being connected to the network and to ensure that these were managed appropriately, in particular through scanning all connected devices.
- E-mail marking – technology was implemented for the e-mail system to allow users to select from a drop-down menu the appropriate marking for the classification of information being sent at a particular instance.
- PC replacement – to continue the work being done on the desktop refresh programme, a dedicated team was

afforded the time to reallocate equipment and ensure that the disposals element was appropriately handled.

- Patch and vulnerability management – a team was required to address the results of the recent penetration testing report and the various patching and server update processes that needed to be done as a matter of urgency.
- E-mail archiving – a solution was implemented to provide quick and searchable e-mail functionality, and retention capabilities that integrated with the existing e-mail system.
- Server farm upgrade – the server infrastructure was upgraded across all of ICT to ensure that the whole server farm met the minimum expected housekeeping levels of ICT operation and information security best practice, in terms of vulnerability assessment and patch management.

As the ISM, you may have no day-to-day authority over the time allocation of resources provided to you on project tasks, and this can be very destabilising in terms of project progress. Of course, the reality, in these straitened financial times, is that it's the same people on each of the project teams. Therefore, setting up sub-projects actually increases their workload as they now have to do even more reporting and upward management, in addition to attending even more meetings. This is very wasteful of time, energy and resources.

Sadly, people never seem to pay attention to the blindingly obvious. So your task has to be to keep highlighting to management that for as long as resources are not afforded appropriate time, the overall project will slip further and further backwards, and they will ultimately pay the price for a lack of compliance with a required external mandate or a lack of connectivity to a particular infrastructure. This would impact a significant number of users, way beyond the immediate management team considerations.

Remember the big picture

Every now and then, you need to take a step back and remind yourself, and everyone else, what it is that you are trying to achieve. Your programme of change is ultimately seeking to influence the review of information flow and business process re-engineering; you have to ensure that any processes undertaken are appropriate, adequate, safe and secure, given the nature of the information assets at risk. This is fundamentally about ensuring your organisation is in compliance with relevant legislation. For example, particularly in the UK, information processing in all its forms must not breach the Data Protection Act, which is from a European Data Protection Directive. Therefore, similar principles apply to all organisations processing information across Europe.

Most endeavours in this area have always been about more than just technology, in spite of their uptake usually being served by the implementation of new tools. It is part and parcel of the information governance agenda, which embraces any legislation, regulation and standard that relates to information as an asset and that requires risk assessment, impact analysis and proper management (we will return to describing the breadth of information governance itself in the next chapter). This, therefore, needs to be owned at a senior level in the organisation and supported with appropriate resources. Otherwise, ICT continues to be perceived as the natural lead, which results in projects being afforded a technical focus rather than an operational one, and users who are left feeling that things are being done *to* them rather than *with* them.

It is certainly true that technological solutions can be used to make the policing and implementation of information security easier, but to ensure the protection of data and information there will always be implications for how we do business. Continuing to deliver on your programme of activity requires changes to policies as well as technology. For example:

- More stringent security checks are required for staff employed by the organisation and these need to be embedded into your personnel-related policies.
- An enhancement to asset management security is usually required, to ensure that all assets are identified across hardware, software and information.
- A meaningful clear-desk policy needs to be in place and adhered to and the acceptable use of ICT services and systems needs to be defined more clearly.
- Information ownership should be established by appointing information asset owners for all systems containing personally identifiable information, in order that such information can be appropriately managed and secured. This should be embedded as a management responsibility.
- Provide all users with some level of information security awareness delivery. This is best achieved through the roll-out of briefings on as many occasions as possible.
- Refresh ICT business continuity arrangements to reflect the updated policies once they define those security requirements.

Breadth of technological change

As mentioned previously, many of the issues addressed by information governance-related programmes of change concern personnel and procedures, but there are obviously technical matters, too. A lot of these have already been covered in previous chapters, but others are identified below:

- Moving users' data to a secure storage area network (SAN) – in our scenario it resulted in data being unavailable to those who were not in the same secure segment of the network.
- Upgrading firewalls, antivirus technology, anti-spam software, routers, switches, cabling, servers, etc. – while this was done for the segmented network, a great deal of work was still required in order to bring the rest of the network up to the expected minimum baseline security standards, as demanded by most external connectivity, regulatory and legislative arrangements.
- Implementing two-factor authentication (2FA) – done in order to address a requirement to identify users reliably. The first factor, 'something you know', is the familiar system password (and as previously described this was upgraded to a mandated minimum eight-character standard), but setting up the second, 'something you have', takes real effort.
- Gathering, storing and presenting security event data is another important part of some external requirements and agreements. This means keeping control over all the security-relevant log data generated by various systems and devices on the network, and putting it into secure storage for future analysis and reporting. Again, there

can be a lot of server work to be done in order to identify, upgrade and maintain this accordingly.

- Implementing a secure network – sadly, not all networks are historically created equal. Most have been created in a segmented manner, cascading across geographical boundaries as organisations grow and system and transactional requirements develop. Achieving the transformation programme requirements for relocating staff and systems can be hampered by old infrastructure, as users may be straddled between secure and insecure platforms, with data housed on different servers in different locations. Adopting a 'one organisation network' usually enables wider transformation and secure information sharing, thus helping the realisation of corporate aims and objectives around information sharing, particularly if you are working in a public sector environment.

- Most external connectivity requirements that are auditable put a high degree of focus on the way services and systems are deployed. Compliance will require corporate commitment to ensure users comply with new regimes surrounding governance of network access, control of the utilisation of hardware and general adherence to associated corporate guidelines and policies.

- Extending the depth of information security across the organisation, accepting it as a BAU activity that benefits from corporate mandate, and embracing management into the information governance culture, are the ultimate goals. In other words, this is how a user culture should always operate, not just for the purposes of gaining connection to a secure network or fulfilling any other contractual, regulatory or legislative requirements.

In reality, anything that is described in this book is nothing more than encouragement to achieve the minimum expected security standards for an organisation.

Embracing data protection and privacy

There is a fundamental and intrinsic link between security and data protection and, indeed, privacy. You cannot have the latter two without the former, and the seventh data protection principle in the UK Data Protection Act defines security as a fundamental requirement to be woven into the fabric of your organisation, ensuring you are in a position to protect personal data in whatever form it might take.

UK Data Protection Act 1998, seventh principle

Appropriate technical and organisational measures shall be taken against unauthorised or unlawful processing of personal data and against accidental loss or destruction of, or damage to, personal data.

As the ISM, it may be that you are asked to assist with fulfilling subject access requests (SARs) when individuals ask to see all the information that your organisation holds on them. This can require trawling through data logs, e-mail archives, system records, etc., as well as paper/manual records, and can be time-consuming and challenging in terms of piecing together the breadth of information captured and ensuring that the response is provided within the requirements of the legislation.

Data protection is a huge legislative learning curve, but it behoves the ISM to learn the Act and understand it from both a legal and technical point of view, as it is not going away. More changes are planned in terms of data breach notification, and the underlying premise in terms of how data protection authority bodies will change too – currently your organisation must handle personal data in a certain way; a) you must know that you have it, b) you must know where it is at all times and c) you must have taken "appropriate technical and organisational measures" to protect that data. The latter, in the 21st century, implies encrypting data at rest, data in motion and data in transit, at a minimum. Again, this is a massive area in itself, and there are many great books that can be found on the subject.

We will address the need to undertake privacy impact assessments (PIAs) in the next chapter. Suffice to say that if you are in this mode of thinking, then you should be able to see the links with business impact assessments or analysis too. The ISM has a key role to play in identifying the likely root causes of threats being realised and establishing their likelihood. Above all, the ISM can write the definition of a great many of the mitigating or compensatory controls that could be implemented to ensure the appropriate protection of personal data and/or information assets, as expected by the regulators, stakeholders and the public at large.

Other security tasks for this month

User administration

This is another easy fix – a low-hanging fruit task – and yet it is so often not addressed. We talked about this back in *Chapter 1*. It is an ongoing task and you really need to make it a mission to ensure that:

- there are no users on the systems who are no longer part of the organisation;
- every single user only has the access they need to do the current job for which they are employed;
- no one is still holding access rights for systems that related to other roles they have previously carried out, for which they no longer require such access.

It's these kinds of little things that really show whether an organisation is taking security seriously, both internally to itself and to outsiders (when audited or otherwise).

Inventory management

The list of items needing to be included on your inventory gets longer and longer, or at least it does if you reflect on the potential risks associated with the use of some machines. Consider the purchase of new dictaphones – the technology has come on so far that these now have an inbuilt storage element similar to a USB drive, and if that drive is not encrypted, you need to review the potential requirement for addressing this risk. What if the dictaphone was dropped in the street? Anyone could pick it up and press play to hear what had been recorded and, depending on the result of the discovery, take it straight to the local media – or worse still, the national press. In all likelihood, this would become an immediate data breach and an incident response would need to swing into action. Mighty oaks from little acorns grow...

Security awareness theme

This month's information security theme could pick up on the fact that the media focus is usually, at least for the first two weeks of February, related to Valentine's Day, so there's a 'love' element. You could run a campaign entitled 'Love your Laptop', where users are encouraged to ensure that they have connected to the network, updated the patches and antivirus status, run a back-up, cleaned out the cookies and Internet history, etc.

Chapter summary

The brevity of this chapter reflects that February always feels like a short month for everyone, depending on how it 'falls' across the calendar weeks. It is a time to make the most of the speed of the month and tackle some of the basics, as have been expressed, while continuing to keep plates spinning at a management level.

CHAPTER 8: MARCH - SLIPPING THROUGH THE NET

The impact of politics

During the period when the core of this research was undertaken, the UK political landscape was changing beyond recognition. In the UK public sector, when an election is forthcoming, there is a time referred to as 'purdah' - the period from when an election is announced until after the election is held, now more often referred to as the pre-election period. There is an immediate hold on spend, no new projects get approved and ultimately money gets clawed back on projects which have already been funded. This results in most employees feeling quite 'stuck', unable to progress existing plans, uncertain of their future – this feeling can be exacerbated depending on the political leaning of their organisation and the likely impact a change of government will have on their future and that of their landscape. Stasis exists.

There will be another one before every general election, so bear this in mind if that's the sector you are in. If you are new in the sector or the role at such a time, it can be quite bewildering as all your planned timelines for delivery of security improvement programmes change suddenly and come to a grinding halt.

This thread will be picked up again in *Chapter 10*.

Privacy impact assessments

In November 2007, the UK public sector approach to data handling turned on its axis as a result of a government department's loss of two CDs. The subsequent months brought forth a relentless number of reviews, inquiries and report outputs, all of which came up with relatively similar conclusions surrounding the need to embed better information security culture, awareness, education, data handling, etc. at all levels across the organisation and the public sector as a whole. As a result new data-handling requirements were required. In November 2008, a year on, the Information Commissioner held a conference entitled 'Privacy by Design' at which he launched the results of some research done (see *www.ico.gov.uk/news/current_topi cs/privacy_by_design_conference.aspx*). The end result was the uptake of the habit of undertaking PIAs as described below.

Definitions

Personal data – This is any data from which a living individual can be identified, whether stand-alone or when combined with other data available to the organisation.

Privacy – The definition of privacy goes beyond personal data to include actions that may intrude on an individual's personal life or affairs. This may include monitoring or screening that will not be held in permanent form.

Benefits of undertaking privacy impact assessment

There are many risks associated with the processes and technology used in the handling of personal data. By identifying risks in the early stages of the project, they can be avoided or mitigated while there is still the opportunity to effect change. Changes made at a later stage or after implementation can be costly, both in financial terms and in damage to reputation.

When any new process or system is proposed, consideration should be given to the impact it may have on the privacy of the stakeholders and, where appropriate, a PIA should be undertaken. Equally, a PIA should be undertaken where significant changes to existing processes or technology are proposed. The assessment involves reviewing proposals in the early stages of the project to identify the privacy risks for all those it may impact upon. Following this, the next step is to document proposed solutions and ways of mitigating privacy risks.

Risks to the individual

These are loss, damage, access or use by unauthorised persons, and personal data being exposed or getting into the public domain. Also, consideration will need to be given to any activity that may contravene the individual's rights.

Risks to the organisation

These are damage to reputation, legal/compensation costs, low adoption of scheme by stakeholders, costs to redesign systems for greater compliance, and collapse of the project or withdrawal of support.

Data considered to be high risk

Sensitive data, as defined in the UK Data Protection Act, can be described in brief as covering health, ethnicity, sexuality, offences, political opinion and trade union membership. More usually, these are listed as:

- racial or ethnic origin;
- political opinions;
- religious beliefs or beliefs of a similar nature;
- membership of a trade union;
- physical or mental health or condition;
- sexual orientation;
- commission or alleged commission of an offence;
- proceedings for any offence or alleged offence, or sentence of court.

There should be an expectation that personal contact information is kept confidential, including e-mail addresses, phone numbers and home address. Other information to be considered includes financial information, details of individuals at risk and travel plans, which could also present risks.

Expected outcomes

These can be expressed as:

- identification of privacy risks;
- understanding of privacy risks from the stakeholders' perspective;
- identification of alternative options;
- understanding of acceptance of the project;
- identification of ways to lessen/avoid negative impacts on privacy;

- where negative impacts are unavoidable, justification for accepting risks;
- documented evidence that privacy has been considered;
- dissolution/cessation of the project, if it is clear that it is not going to meet legal obligations or compliance requirements, or if is not going to be possible to maintain the appropriate and expected levels of security and privacy for the individuals' personal data involved.

All of these can be incredibly important and valuable, depending on who the audience is and who your stakeholders are.

To enable the assessment to take place, the following information must be gathered.

Conducting a privacy impact assessment

All groups who may have an interest in, or be affected by, the project should be identified, with a brief description of their role and the nature of any likely impact.

Carry out an environmental scan. Learn from other projects, whether internal or in the wider external environment. Useful sources include:

- project documentation for previous projects, including LLLs (especially where the project is aimed at replacing existing technology);
- reports, articles and papers in the public domain;
- discussions with others with expertise in the project area or with knowledge of compliance issues;
- when purchasing new technology, discussions with reference sites may provide information on how they have addressed privacy issues.

In most circumstances, for projects which involve personal data, a small-scale assessment will be appropriate. Examples of projects where a small-scale assessment would be appropriate include:

- replacing an existing personal data system with new software;
- design and development of a system where the data held is on a consent basis;
- changes to an existing system, where additional personal data will be collected;
- a proposal to collect personal data from a new source;
- creation or redesign of web forms for collecting personal data;
- development of new procedures for authentication;
- plans to outsource business processes involving storing and processing personal data;
- developing or amending policy statements relating to staff usage of council-provided technology, e.g. mobile phones and laptops.

A full-scale assessment should only be considered where there is likely to be considerable impact on your organisation's handling of personal data, including one or more of the following activities:

- use of technologies that could impact on privacy;
- use of sensitive personal data (as defined in the Data Protection Act, e.g. race or ethnic origin, health, political opinion, religion, offences, sexuality);
- use of confidential information or information which could be used for identity theft, e.g. bank account details or other financial information;

- use of excessive authentication data, e.g. biometrics (fingerprints or iris scans) or copies of birth certificates or similar documentation;
- publication of unprotected personal data without consent;
- sharing of sensitive data with third-party organisations;
- holding of large quantities of personal data relating to an individual;
- holding personal data relating to a large number of individuals.

Conducting a small-scale privacy impact assessment

The following phases are recommended in the Information Commissioner's guidance:

- **Preparation phase:** make arrangements for a consultation exercise. Identify the main stakeholders and develop a consultation strategy/plan. In small-scale projects, this may not need to be formalised.
- **Consultation and analysis phase:** discuss privacy issues with key stakeholders to enable the identification of the main risks to privacy. This phase also includes the identification of possible solutions. Consultation can, in some circumstances, be on a small scale, e.g. e-mailing key stakeholders for their views.
- **Documentation phase:** record the outcomes of the analysis, either in report format or by using a checklist, with any relevant documented information attached. Alternatively, risks and solutions can be included in a project risk register, where available.
- **Review phase:** any recommendations should have a brought-forward time, in which the documentation

should be reviewed to ensure that the solutions have been put into effect and to review the success of such measures. Any new aspects to the project should also be reviewed to ensure that they do not impact on privacy.

Compliance with legislation and regulations

In addition to the PIA, the project owner/leader must ensure that the project is compliant with relevant legislation including:

- Data Protection Act 1998
- Human Rights Act 1998
- Regulation of Investigatory Powers 2000 (RIPA)
- Privacy and Electronic Communications Regulations 2003
- Sector legislation and Codes of Practice

Other legislative considerations in the UK include:

- Anti-terrorism, Crime and Security Act, Section 11 – Retention of Communications Data 2001
- Civil Contingencies Act 2004
- Computer Misuse Act 1990
- Copyright, Designs and Patents Act 1988
- Criminal Justice and Immigration Act 2008
- Defamation Act 1996
- Electronic Communications Act 2000
- Environmental Information Regulations 2004 (EIR)
- Freedom of Information Act 2000
- Government Connect Code of Connection (CoCo)
- Obscene Publications Act 1959 & 1964
- Payment Card Industry Data Security Standard (PCI DSS)

- Waste Electrical & Electronics Equipment (WEEE) directive.

Across the globe, there is a plethora of information-led legislative statutes that apply to organisations, and the ISM role includes the need to identify these and document them for reference and compliance purposes.

There seems to be a tendency for those who bury their security function in ICT to have a very narrow view of what compliance means. It is far beyond complying with a technical control, like a firewall rule set. It is this and so much more – compliance with all policies, procedures and guidelines as required by the legislative, regulatory and statutory frameworks to which your organisation, in whatever sector it is based, is expected to adhere.

Addressing privacy risks

By addressing privacy risks up front in any new system development or process change, your organisation can avoid the risk of falling foul of the applicable data protection legislation:

- Minimising data collection to information necessary for a specified purpose, and restricting its use for that purpose, is an important strategy. If you don't hold the information in the first place, you can mitigate your risks by not recording it at all.
- Eliminating collection of contentious data is another, i.e. blocking the use of particular information for decision making.
- Non-collection of biometric data for authentication is another.

- Delete or destroy data on completion of transactions for which it was required – this is best achieved through the application of retention and destruction schedules (in conjunction with RM).

It's important to use your organisation's complaints process to determine avoidance and mitigation measures. You can easily identify trends when you see what people are complaining about. Ask for a review of a few months' worth of external complaints, as well as internal user complaints. There is often some gold to be sifted therein. Users can spot when there is too much data being asked for on new forms, or are aware of historic forms where the data is never required or never used in any meaningful way. It needs to be part of your communication strategy to engage in this way as it becomes part of your risk mitigation.

A PIA can be carried out at any point on existing systems, too, so that you have one as evidence that the above considerations have been dealt with. You could schedule this for corporate systems, in particular, throughout the year so that you are able to refer to the outputs and update them annually in case there have been any external legislative or regulatory changes, or internal system or process changes.

Managing a virus outbreak

Remember Conficker? It was painful if you experienced it in your organisation – and the instant response, as with any major virus outbreak, is to keep quiet. But you need to take action, so you have to get people involved, in particular, in locking down the offending machine(s) and patching like crazy! Given that your users can just as easily leak information to the outside as anyone else, handling communications becomes part of your ISM role and needs to be done very carefully. Upwards management amongst you and your teams internally, as well as across a large organisation, takes staging and resourcing, too.

Obviously we've talked about the requirements for patch management and vulnerability assessments. An outbreak like this is your chickens coming home to roost, as it is the most obvious result of a lack of housekeeping. The first patch for Conficker was issued in October 2008, so to be experiencing it in your network in 2010, and to be exposed, was pretty embarrassing and told quite a tale in itself. While the child in you desperately wants to shout from the rooftops 'I told you so', it obviously isn't the polite, politically correct or job-enhancing response, so tread lightly!

We found, through some rapid network analysis, that there were many devices showing they had the hotfixes for Conficker applied. But it was hard to gauge whether the data being presented was wholly accurate and whether all the servers and other hosts were present, given there was a gap between the known total number of devices and the number of devices analysed. (Back to my *Chapter 1* checklist of tasks – it is vital that you have that inventory of your estate accurate and up to date at all times, for just this kind of eventuality.) The scan across the network only picks up what is visible in the configuration management system and, thus, if it is not visible, it is not captured and the network may be exposed.

NT4 had no patch against Conficker because, of course, it was on Microsoft's planned unsupported software listing and, therefore, there were no plans to bother with it. So, at the time, if you were still hosting NT4 machines (and they still exist out there to this day) then they were at risk of virus exposure.

The IPS was generating warnings from a host network obfuscating behind the proxy and DNS. This is odd behaviour and indicative of the creative nature of the malware itself. Finding the host was the first task, as it was sending out replication messages across the network for as long as it was allowed to broadcast a signal.

So, what do you do if a significant part of your estate has not yet been updated? It transpired that there were, in fact, quite a number of servers that had not been audited because the antivirus system had been turned off. The antivirus technology stops communicating if it is not updated, and the users needed to be set up in appropriate groups to have their local machines updated. In spite of these glaring compounded risks, decisions needed to be made urgently in order to get to a position where the antivirus system could be put back on, across the whole network.

While turning off the technical solution may solve one problem, for a short period of time, it may create another risk. In panic mode, there will always be impractical considerations with regard to what could be done manually and technically, so your role as ISM is to maintain a level head and manage the teams and resources necessary to achieve a satisfactory outcome for all.

Applying hotfixes across a WAN can be tricky, but is part of your solution set and again requires some planning in order to ensure that users leave their machines in the appropriate 'switched on' state to allow for the application of the hotfix. This relates back to our discussion in *Chapter 5* about needing to be aligned with the IT folk addressing 'green' IT, whereby they would be seeking to ensure that machines were switched off every evening. Co-ordination and communication were going to be required in order to achieve the desired outcome on this one (as with all other tasks and challenges).

Other information security tasks this month

Maintain a lively and trustworthy intranet presence

You need an interactive intranet that is regularly updated with useful information – FAQs and guides, as well as policy documentation – so that people know that there is a trusted source of information. Seed this with an equivalent RSS feed of daily news items that reflect issues that are bound up in good information security practice, or are evidence of why it needs to be in place. Most breaches are reflective of 'there but for the grace of whoever you worship go the rest of us'. Often it is only a matter of time – no one can be complacent and the larger your organisation, the greater the risk of an ill-informed user making a human error – without meaning or malice, it's just the reality of the law of averages.

Things we were asked for included 'Instant Astrologer' and access to 'www.mates.com' … um, really?

Inventory management (again)

I thought I'd heard it all with the dictaphones query, until I was asked what we were doing about camcorders! Somewhere, in the many lists of things you need to keep juggling and spinning as an ISM, you need to have an overview, for each team, section, department and directorate, of what their function is and what type of equipment you should therefore expect them to need. Your colleagues in the RM area could already be gathering this kind of information, as it should be picked up under 'what media do you use to capture, use, share and store information?' Either way, you need to be able to research the requirements and to help design the most appropriately secure solution.

Security awareness theme

This month's information security theme could pick up on any subject of your choice. In this particular example and with experience from the chapter, tackling antivirus best practice would be the obvious choice! As long as you encourage the users to ensure that they update their own antivirus product on their home machines, they will appreciate the scale of the effort you will be applying across your whole organisation when it comes to protection mechanisms.

Chapter summary

This chapter has, in particular, focused on the mechanisms that constitute a PIA process. This has been done in order to help the ISM appreciate the role they play in steering the organisation to conduct such assessments and keep track of the results on an ongoing basis.

CHAPTER 9: APRIL - LINKING INFOSEC WITH INFOGOV

A linguistic journey to information governance

As we've established, the information security industry loves its acronyms and abbreviations, so in this instance we have InfoSec for information security, and for information governance we have InfoGov.

As an ISM you need to be thinking more broadly, as this is the trajectory at the moment. Information security begets information assurance begets information governance. If we are truly protecting information assets, holistically, this is where we will end up. So, be prepared to think more widely than your current scope of understanding, and do a lot of reading and extra learning.

We have seen other acronyms in our space, including GRC (governance, risk and compliance) - but we need to really start getting to grips with the meaning of the words that make up these acronyms. Governance is supposed to mean visibility of governance across the whole organisation. Risk, in this instance, is again supposed to mean risk management across the organisation, not just specifically IT risk. Business risk, financial risk, reputational risk, information risk – they all need to be dealt with holistically. Finally, the compliance aspect of this triangle requires an appreciation of the whole legislative, regulatory and standards requirements for your organisation, not just compliance with a firewall policy. It is far beyond this. It is compliance with everything that we have been talking about in this book, all the policies, procedures, standards and guidelines combined. This is because they should have been crafted with an understanding of the compliance landscape so that you can evidence that you are complying with everything required of you.

The international standard ISO/IEC 38500:2008 described the corporate governance of IT as being "the system by which the current and future use of IT is directed and controlled". Corporate governance of IT involves evaluating and directing the use of IT to support the organisation, and monitoring this use to achieve plans. It includes the strategy and policies for using IT within an organisation. However, what we are talking in this chapter are the links from information security to information governance. This takes IT governance to the next level, beyond just the technology, in keeping with all the movements over the last few years across 'big data/raw data', the *information spring* if you will. What is required is a holistic view. So let's take a journey through the various stages from IT security through to information governance.

How did we get here?

Research can show that the journey to IA, which precedes information governance, is via the following themes that have emerged over time:

- physical security;
- operational security (OpSec);
- computer security (CompuSec);
- communications security (ComSec);
- IT security (ITSec);
- information systems security (InfoSec), which merged ComSec and CompuSec following rapid changes in technology and, thus, combined in a new paradigm to

become InfoSec, internationally recognised in the Common Criteria for Information Technology Security Evaluation Protection Profiles (*see www.commoncriteriaportal.org/*);

- system safety;
- system reliability.

System safety is not something that we have found ourselves focusing on to any great extent in the information security industry, although there are a number of publications that put it squarely inside our boundaries. In many ways, this is a better lens through which to view things, as it provides a broader perspective. It also shows why we must provide the high levels of protection that we are seeking after risk assessments. The classic triad of 'CIA' was originally a ComSec definition covering:

- Confidentiality of information: ensuring it is accessible only to those authorised to have access and ensuring data is kept private whether manual or electronic.
- Integrity of information: safeguarding the accuracy (inputs and outputs) and completeness of information through the application of controls and management checks.
- Availability of information: ensuring that only authorised users have access to information when required during its life cycle; making sure information stays in the right hands, in the right place, at the right time.

In 1991, John McCumber presented a pedagogic framework at the National Computer Security Conference on this subject and highlighted the constituent parts of InfoSec, including the need for a 'common language/terminology in order to communicate effectively'. The model embraced the need to embed the people, process and technology triad as an overlay on the three main goals of security (achieving the CIA of the information you are seeking to protect). McCumber articulated these as "Education, Training and Awareness (people); Policy and Practices (process) and Technology". (McCumber, 1991 and 2004) The original model, presented by McCumber, for InfoSec, is shown in *Figure 6*.

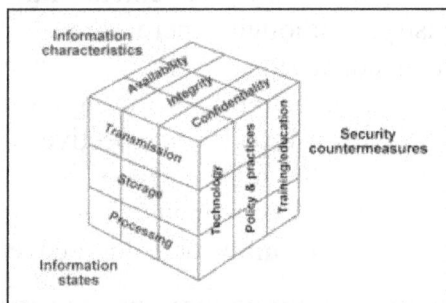

Figure 6: Model of three main security goals
(source: McCumber, 1991)

So, InfoSec was very much about the integration of personnel security, computer security, communications security and operational security into an identifiable profession. InfoSec "in any language, in any culture, in any country" is relative to the protection of those information systems. (Kovacich, 1998)

A decade after McCumber's InfoSec model was described, there was an update in the form of a seminal paper that articulated the definition and direction of IA for the coming years. Maconachy, working at the US National Security Agency at the time, saw IA as embracing the triad of information security; but he believed it needed to be articulated in terms of four dimensions (Maconachy *et al*, 2001):

- Information states – can be aligned with protective marking classifications and types in the UK.
- Security services – these are the five pillars.
- Security countermeasures – we refer to these as controls or safeguards in the UK, embracing people, process and technology aspects.
- Time – this aligns with the security development life cycle as our information is in constant flux dependent upon time.

Information assurance should be viewed as "both multidisciplinary and multidimensional". The dimensions are represented as information states, security countermeasures and security services – and these are all understood to be affected by time. Information can have a greater sensitivity, depending on when it is produced or released. Information assurance is both art and science, so it needs to be tackled through multidisciplinary efforts (Petersen *et al*, 2004).

The information states can also be overlaid with the following approach: creating information profiles that correspond to levels of protection required for information (UK CESG, Protection Profiles), which in turn correspond with the likely countermeasures to be implemented in the solution space:

- (being) aware (medium)
- deter (medium-high)
- detect and resist (high)
- defend (very high)

In 2002, Debra Herrmann proposed a broader definition of IA as an engineering discipline that cuts across the safety domain, and some 10 years on we are finally seeing some real traction in this safety space.

Herrmann contended that a "safe, reliable and secure system by definition has proactively built-in error/fault/failure (whether accidental or intentional) prevention, detection, containment, and recovery mechanisms" (Herrmann, 2002, p.9). Herrmann saw IA as a three-dimensional challenge, encompassing "safety, reliability and security". This book should be mandatory reading for all IA professionals across the UK!

The most fulsome and concise definition of IA can be found in a US Air Force instruction bulletin (US Department of the Air Force, 2001) which describes IA in terms of information operations (military language) and includes reference to the need to also be able to restore systems and how to do so. This means you need to be able to protect, detect and react to situations:

Information operations that protect and defend information and information systems by ensuring their availability, integrity, authentication, confidentiality, and non-repudiation. This includes providing for restoration of information systems by incorporating protection, detection, and reaction capabilities. (US Department of the Air Force, 2001)

Most other US Department of Defense publications also refer to the same definition (NIST, CNSS, CNSSI, etc.).

Separating out what the term 'information' refers to is key to understanding IA. For example, the function and responsibility of an organisation's security personnel are to protect corporate assets. Information systems and the information that they store, process and transmit are some of the most valuable assets. Information assurance includes those actions that protect and defend information and information systems.

Information assurance should be seen as both a business enabler and a business protector, ensuring that users of information systems are not unwittingly exposing themselves to unacceptable risk. This has also been expressed as IA representing a migration from a preventative approach to an enabling approach (McFadzean, 2005).

A combination of this thinking was then brought from the US to the UK by the independent partnership organisation – the Information Assurance Advisory Council (IAAC) – who described IA as follows:

Information Assurance is the certainty that the information within an organisation is reliable, secure and private. IA encompasses both the accuracy of the information and its protection, and includes disciplines such as information security management, risk management and business continuity management. (IAAC, 2003)

Information is fundamental to the business of government. Effective IA is at the core of ensuring that this asset is safeguarded appropriately. The continued growth throughout government of the use of ICT systems, all linked together, carries with it increased vulnerability. In addition, these ICT systems are under threat of attack from foreign intelligence services, criminal gangs, and even individuals inside the organisation.

Information security in itself requires controls to be implemented, the best of which are preventive (in the most obvious sense of preventing any breach of security from taking place in the first instance). These are elements which form the basic components of security architecture, for example, firewalls, user access control mechanisms, encryption of data and communications, digital signatures and data back-up systems, and detective controls, such as IDSs or security monitoring platforms. The various technical controls are usually complemented by a framework of security policies, procedures and guidelines aimed at controlling the actions of the users to whom the framework applies.

This was at a time when the discourse of the period was beginning to change, as departmental IT went through the push and pull of decentralisation and the struggle to manage information assets really began, as Wylder pointed out (Wylder, 2004, p.21).

Wylder's writing is some of the most comprehensive at the time, with regard to the breadth and depth of information security and what a professional should be doing in terms of their role.

There are a number of basic steps that are found sequentially in most information security standards (ISO27001, ISACA BMIS, etc.), which build towards the identification and implementation of an ISMS (Dimitriadis, 2011). These are:

- Business impact analysis – looking at the impact on the business following the appearance of a threat, usually in terms of the monetary, reputation or legal impact.
- Risk analysis – the possibility of the occurrence of a security incident is calculated, based on a database of security weaknesses. This step needs to take into account technical controls that are already in place to reduce risk and any other complementary controls already available.

- Risk management – once identified, the risks are prioritised in relation to the impact level and business appetite for risk.
- ISMS implementation – this is a robust management framework implementation, including consideration of human, cultural, technical, business and external factors, and requires metrics, measurement and continuous improvements.

Unfortunately, what we have ended up experiencing in implementation terms is a lack of consistency, as each sector, industry and organisation has appeared to implement security on the basis of their specific business needs and created different security definitions to suit themselves.

As mentioned earlier, IA must be maintained throughout the life cycle of a system; threats change with the changing political or business environment; vulnerabilities appear and disappear as the configuration of the system changes and new weaknesses are discovered; and the impact of systems failure changes as dependency on a system develops. This is where CESG (the UK Government's Communications-Electronics Security Group, known formally as CESG) come in with the various accreditation schemes, etc. (UK CESG, Certification).

Often security is thought of as an event rather than a process, as a stitch in time rather than a thread that runs throughout each phase of a system's life cycle. Security is often not considered during the initial planning, design and development of the system. Attempts to retrofit security into the system after it is developed are typically more expensive and less effective than if it is incorporated from inception. Likewise, security does not end once the system has been accredited and approved to operate under certain conditions. Throughout the system's operational and maintenance phase, the system's compliance with the terms of its accreditation must be verified. Even when the system's life cycle is over, security policies and procedures must govern the secure destruction and disposal of the system. (Boyce and Jennings, 2002, p.170)

It can be shown that in the UK, IA broadens out to include data protection and privacy (because of the close confidentiality links and the Organisation for Economic Co-operation and Development (OECD) guidance requirements), information management and quality, records management, and much more. However, the assurance function cannot be deployed until the risks are fully understood (Schou and Shoemaker, 2007, p.13). The OECD guidance clearly states that the "use of an information system and its security should respect the legitimate rights and interests of others and should be compatible with the legitimate use and flow of data and information in a democratic society". That requirement has not diminished, rather increasing in importance in the past two decades.

In the late 1990s, the term IA was known only by small groups of security experts, often considered to be 'paranoid' or 'rigid'. Today, IA is well known by a much wider audience involved with public sector projects and contracts, ranging from high-level executives to engineers in many disciplines. Many have sought information on IA processes through reading papers and attending briefings. Yet even in the late 2000s it appeared that the status quo was very similar, with only a small number of professionals truly understanding the breadth of meaning and the scale of available material upon which to draw experience, understanding and wisdom (Hutton, 2008).

Today, you can choose from 'information security', 'information risk', 'information risk management', 'information protection' or 'information assurance' and also the US-centric, all-embracing umbrella of "governance, risk and compliance (GRC)" (Tone at the Top, 2010). GRC, itself is prone to as many as 22 different definitions (Marks, 2011), although the most favoured is that provided by the Open Compliance and Ethics Group (OCEG, 2011). Fundamentally, GRC is not about technology, but about business processes and doing them better. It is a lens through which an organisation can understand their business and appreciate why these elements need to work together in harmony (risk management and strategy), addressing fragmented processes, removing silos and working pan-organisationally. The international standard for risk management, ISO31000, provides a definition and is of value in this context (British Standards Institution, 2009).

The goal is to transform information security into a multidisciplinary field in which technologists work closely with experts in 'soft issues', such as public policy, economics and sociology (Shostack and Stewart, 2008, p.103). ISACA picked up this concept well in their Business Model for Information Security (*see Figure 7*), seeking to provide an "in-depth explanation to a holistic business model which examines security issues from a systems perspective" (ISACA, 2009).

Even if you do not like the term 'information assurance' it has a long history, which clearly not enough people are aware of; so this section seeks to put the pieces together. It can be seen from what is widely available in published form that IA is often used as a synonym for security (Boyce and Jennings, 2002). While it may be that "attempts to create strictly defined vocabulary within information security are likely doomed to failure as long as English remains a living language" (Shostack and Stewart, 2008), it is important to appreciate that practical issues flow from definitions. Security may historically have been an IT issue, but assurance raises the bar to a much more organisational issue which, given the importance of valuing information as an asset and the need to protect both reputation and personal privacy, clearly shows the breadth of the requirement.

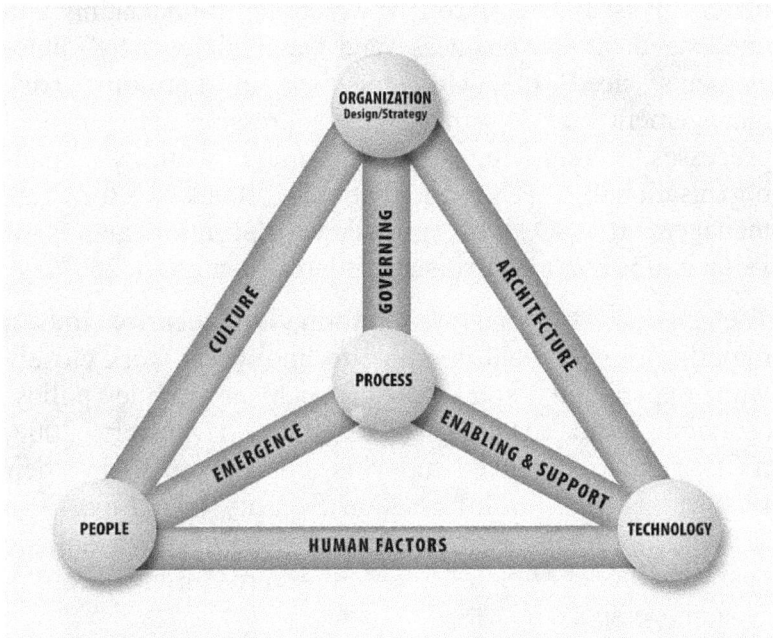

Figure 7: ISACA BMIS – business model for information security

From IA to IG

Putting IA and InfoSec together, you actually get 'information governance' (IG or InfoGov). InfoGov is the set of multidisciplinary structures, policies, procedures, processes and controls implemented to manage information on all media in such a way that they support an organisation's immediate and future regulatory, legal, risk, environmental and operational requirements. This includes information held in every form (information systems, on paper, other records). It is underpinned by a management process that takes a co-ordinated approach to information assets across an organisation. It embraces information management, including information security management, information and records management, data protection, privacy (because of close confidentiality links and the OECD guidance requirements) and physical protection. It includes aspects of corporate governance, risk management and business continuity, and must be maintained throughout an organisation's life cycle in the face of changing threats, vulnerabilities and dependencies.

Central to IG is an understanding of the journey from IT security, through information security, to IA – all of which are about maturing to a position of being able to demonstrate justified confidence in security measures, processes and practices in the management of information. While IA has been seen to be the growth area in recent years, maturing out of information security, the ultimate goal must be to embed a full IG framework across all organisations in order to fully include the total breadth of information-related legislation, regulation, standards, policies, procedures, technology and people issues that need to be managed, handled and protected in today's cyber-dominated environment.

Consider, if you will, the '11 Cs' of IG.

Eleven Cs of IG:

1 centralisation
2 communication
3 (legislative) compliance
4 confidence
5 confidentiality (integrity, availability)
6 conformance
7 consistency
8 content
9 continuity
10 (security) controls
11 corporate records management.

(And now for something completely different…! For those of a spiritual nature, apparently the number 11 possesses the qualities of intuition, patience, honesty, sensitivity, and spirituality, and is idealistic. People turn to those who have these '11' qualities for teaching and inspiration, and are usually uplifted by the experience. Not for nothing, nor randomly, are these things chosen!)

Your aim as an ISM should be to seek a deeper understanding of IG and the principles for good information management and handling, enabling technologies and current best practices and, at the same time, to gain a broad appreciation of the many facets of the information at the heart of all that you will encounter.

At a minimum, over time, you could consider your body of knowledge to ensure you have a broad understanding across all of these areas:

- principles of IA and beyond
- standards and best-practice management of information security (BP)
- software assurance (SA)
- data protection and privacy (DP)
- records management (RM)
- business continuity/disaster recovery/resilience (BC).

Table 6: Areas of knowledge required

Information assurance principles & beyond (IA)	Data protection & privacy (DP)
<ul><li>Information governance overview</li><li>Information governance framework</li><li>Information assurance – history – how did we get here?</li><li>Overview of relevant information-based legislation</li><li>Data-handling review and other government-led initiatives</li><li>Information assurance maturity model (IAMM)</li><li>Culture, ethics and professionalism</li><li>Internal and external audit</li></ul>	<ul><li>Data protection principles</li><li>Maintaining public trust and respecting personal privacy</li><li>Information sharing/data transfers – benefits and constraints</li><li>Privacy impact assessments</li><li>Gaining consent, direct marketing</li><li>Managing cookies</li><li>Data-quality management</li><li>Data-breach management – and links to security incident management</li><li>Data protection in the workplace</li><li>Use of personal data in system testing</li><li>Criminal offences and the ICO's power to fine</li><li>Handling subject access</li></ul>

	requests (SARs) • Binding corporate rules • PIMS and BS10012
Standards and best-practice management of information security (BP)	**Records management (RM)**
• Information risk management (IRM) • Risk appetite and risk culture • Governance, risk and compliance (GRC) • ISO27001 and ISMS • Payment card industry data security standard (PCI DSS) • COBIT, COSO, ITIL	• Records management programme (RMP) • Records and information management (RIM) • Standards (ISO15489) and compliance • Vital and historic records • Archives, destruction, retention schedules • Handling records in mergers and acquisitions • RM requirements in system decommissioning • RM links with DR and back-up • RM links with e-mail management and archiving • RM links with file plan and directory structures
Software assurance (SA)	**Business continuity/ disaster recovery/ resilience (BC)**
• How cybersecurity fits in • Threats and vulnerability analysis • Security controls (access control models and	• Including information security in the business continuity management process • Business continuity and risk assessment • Business continuity planning

mechanisms) • Usable security • Designing security in • Firewalls and data encryption • Privacy enhancing technologies • Defence in depth • Cryptography • Identity management • Human factors in security design	framework, BS25999 • Business impact analysis • Testing, maintaining and reassessing business continuity plans • Selecting, developing and implementing DR plans • Embedding a resilience strategy • Addressing counter-terrorism in the planning

Other security tasks for this month

Addressing user requirements

We had a need to revoke CD auto-enable on our PC build in order to achieve a government-dictated security requirement. However, sometime later a request was received by ICT to switch the auto-run feature back on as the users were finding it too challenging (I'm being polite) to perform the sequence required: 'Windows®, Computer, double-click on the external USB drive'! Given that this would mean having to raise an exception to a policy, careful communication and explanation was required in order to ensure that the status quo could be maintained without causing too much angst for the users.

Addressing old equipment requirements

We've seen over the months that there are various requirements for assisting in what might be considered to be tasks related to facilities management. The reason for your apparent 'meddling' is to ensure that you are actually providing the right level of care and attention to the end-of-life stage of equipment, given that your whole life cycle demands this kind of approach. So, when a user comes forward with a large box of old disks, what do we do with them? The users says they are fine to be disposed of, but how do we know what is on them, so that we can justify the decision to destroy them? It would be a laborious task to review all the disks. Every day is filled with this kind of conundrum to be solved. Perhaps a random sampling of the contents could be done – if the disks are still machine readable – and then a level of judgement applied as to whether or not the information in its entirety is actually past its retention period. Engage with the RM team, whenever possible, so that they can make the appropriate amendments to the RM systems that should be recording such information. As long as you have some evidence for the actions taken and justification for the approach, it will be easy enough to explain yourself, should anyone question this further down the line.

Ongoing antivirus management

When your organisation experiences a serious virus (malware) outbreak, it can be a pretty defining moment for the ISM. The team was still trying to contain the Conficker attack, which had spread still further as a result of the lack of previous management of the servers (as highlighted in the penetration test results report). The extent of the damage was eventually realised when a brute-force attack was identified on a server. This was immediately isolated from the network, but it needed to be patched and this brought forward some real thorny issues of:

- why servers were not being patched;
- which ones were in or out of a management loop;
- how long it takes to make decisions about patching and updating these servers. The demonstration of how easily and quickly you can get exposed, and how it is likely to play out in the public perception if the media get hold of the news, showed how inadequate the patching process was.

Security metrics

Statistics, metrics and measurements – call them what you will, but you really need to get your head around them in order to be able to provide management with something tangible, be it a list or a picture with a pie chart or graph. People need to see things either improving or not, with answers or explanations for the latter and options for returning to a state of improvement. As the ISO set about creating the numbering scheme for information security management, ISO27000, it allowed for a lot of supporting standards. So we now have 'ISO/IEC 27004:2009 Information Technology – Security Techniques – Information Security Management – Measurement'.

There are also several existing maturity models that can be adapted to suit your needs. In the UK public sector, there is a more than adequate IA maturity model, which is supported by an IA assessment framework to help assess your progress towards achieving the required level of maturity. (Available at *www.cesg.gov.uk/Pages/Search.asp x?k=Information%20Assurance%20Maturity%20Model*.)

Most maturity models adopt the phased approach of grading, from no implementation to embedded. In this case (IAMM), the gradings are as follows:

- Level 1 – initial
- Level 2 – established
- Level 3 – business enabling
- Level 4 – quantitatively managed
- Level 5 – optimised.

Adopting an accepted framework relevant to your industry helps to benchmark your starting point and provides a trajectory of expected progress. This is something well worth considering from as early on as is possible in your role. You then have a level of tangibility in your management reporting and can provide graphical or pictorial representation of the current status of information security in your organisation. Think of it as seeking to provide a 'confidence count' – how confident you are in the data that is being collected, the way in which it is currently being represented and the way in which it could be represented to better tell the story of information security implementation and its onward journey.

Managing a more security-aware user population

The most applicable phrase here has to be 'be careful what you wish for'. The more you heighten awareness, the more you are likely to garner responses and input from your user base. When you run regular information security awareness briefings, people feel more able to talk about issues of concern regarding information security and data protection.

And now for a completely random user share!

A concerned employee, after experiencing my open style of delivering an information security awareness briefing session, i.e. having her eyes opened, took me aside with a query. Following the sad and tragic loss of a baby, should the university have contacted her, researching how this made her feel, without reference to any data protection/privacy statement? All it did was bring the incident back to the fore for the poor individual and upset them all over again. Greater care and caution is required, as the legal phrase in question is 'damage and distress'. When an individual is stood before you, querying whether this should ever have happened to them, you're presented with a powerful example. But in terms of the bigger picture, they certainly learnt more about the legislative wrap-around that does exist and so they know that they have a recourse in the future.

People also started to notice the little things when it came to system development, like passwords being displayed in a field on the screen in clear text, and they took the time and trouble to report these kinds of findings to the ISM, who then would have to come up with a solution and provide some feedback. The information security standards are developed on the basis of an understanding of the 'plan, do, check, act' loop – where you *plan* to do something, *do* it, *check* if it's working and *act* if it isn't. So the user feedback is vital to allow you to *act* if things are not working as expected.

The 'cut and paste' facility was worrying a lot of users as they realised that this could be a huge risk, given the nature of the information that could easily be copied out of corporate systems. This needed to be monitored in terms of the number of applications that allowed it and the likely level of information contained in those systems. This might be leaking out as a result of users trying to be helpful, cutting and pasting information from a corporate, secure, sensitive system into an e-mail, to exchange with colleagues in other third-party locations in order to fast-track solutions.

Following delivery of another information security awareness briefing in an outlying office location, a laptop 'appeared' from under a desk. It clearly hadn't been used in weeks, so was locked out of the hard-disk encryption tool. As an ISM, you need to decide whether or not you are going to start to report every one of these kinds of breach as an 'incident' in the appropriate system, as it can be very useful for both planning and management visibility – particularly in explaining what it is you have been getting up to!

Security awareness theme

This month's information security theme should usually be focusing on Easter, as it occurs at this time. You could run a campaign whereby you leave chocolates (mini eggs, for example, to keep in theme!) on the desks of those users who are adhering to your clear-desk policy.

Chapter summary

This chapter has very much focused on a journey through the history of the various terms that populate the industry, to help the ISM understand their role in all things information. While it may feel like the end result is greater confusion, the chapter can be used for reference on an ongoing basis, depending on the needs that arise as your role grows and you become embedded in your organisation.

Much like any other profession, there will be many who will disagree with the way these definitions have been represented, but the author would challenge their research and depth of reading!

CHAPTER 10: MAY - POLITICS AND MANAGEMENT

Situational political awareness

Wikipedia describes 'situational awareness' as:

The perception of environmental elements with respect to time and/or space, the comprehension of their meaning, and the projection of their status after some variable has changed, such as time... It is also a field of study concerned with perception of the environment critical to decision-makers in complex, dynamic areas.

In many ways, the construction of this book is about pulling together a lot of elements that are important to the ISM role because they help you to maintain your situational awareness. An understanding of the impact of politics is part of that jigsaw.

This was the month of a change of government in the UK, which had a profound impact on the whole of the public sector ICT infrastructure and strategy planning for quite some time. While the arrival of the new government (Conservative–Liberal alliance) should have heralded momentum, it did not transpire that way, particularly because of the tremendous recession and economic turmoil that was having a lasting impact.

The new government of the day planned to scrap some £15bn of controversial IT projects, including the ID card scheme and the national identity register (£4bn), the next generation of biometric passports and the contact point database (£224m). This was to have a significant impact on a number of working plans at the time related to authentication of users on systems and information sharing out of some of those systems.

A great deal of the intended focus was on transparency and the 'right to government data' which turned into the UK's effort at 'big data' and 'raw data', as well as the publication of all local government spending over £500 and the publishing online of all government tender documents, etc. All of this had huge implications for the IT engine room of organisations involved in such work, as well as for the InfoSec-related controls and safeguards that had been building up over time. As the intention was to publish a large swathe of information that had hitherto been under wraps, risk assessments would be needed to judge the impact and to address issues of data quality, integrity, accuracy and presentation. This was the start of a mammoth undertaking for all concerned. While entirely worthy as a public sector goal, it was not without its overheads and represented a significant distraction from what was already a full workload with depleting resources.

Language and management challenges

It can often be the case that managers appear not to be paying attention because their perception is that security is getting in the way. Information security is accused of stifling innovation. This is an unfair representation of the reality when you take an objective look at the situation.

Failure to consider the time and motion costs of stopping projects, clawing back money and then reigniting the work at a later stage are costing organisations (the public sector, in particular) dearly. Capitalisation of the funding for projects is also the wrong view, as ICT can then find itself running out of funding for its own department. This can be a risky strategy, given the need for ICT to be the firm and secure bedrock upon which the organisation is founded.

There are obviously time and cost considerations when implementing all the latest technologies. Just because one lone powerful enthusiast in your ICT department is allowed to do so – without engaging the business or fully understanding or appreciating the business processes that the technologies were seeking to support, nor risk-assessing the impacts, threats and vulnerabilities – does not make it right or wise. You need to watch out for this.

'I don't understand what's involved in hardening a server', said the individual ultimately responsible for the relevant ICT function. On one hand, this was a very honest admission, but on the other was an appalling reality. But it is probably very likely the case, many times over in many organisations, as security continues to be so little understood by the ICT profession. However, as none of the staff underneath the individual had the skills to 'manage upwards', nor were they motivated to go away and find out more about the challenges, this key issue was left constantly floundering.

Several staff attended a security certification course and thereafter understood that a key phrase to use was 'does the business accept the risk?' But while they were happy 'throwing it out there', there was no mechanism to find out whether or not the business did or did not accept the risk – or even understand it.

'Why am I doing licensing?' asked the person whose responsibility it was, even though they knew they were the only one with the appropriate software licensing qualification (FAST). You need to check your licences, as you could be spending money on licences for products that the users will never need or have no training for and, thus, will never use. Either way, there are cost implications.

A senior director left in a hurry and those underneath were then left with little or no faith in the continuity of the change programme, its sustainability or financial support. Consultants were being brought in at director level and were blocking progress because they were new and frequently needed to find out everything from scratch. This is a constant and classic organisational problem, where skills and knowledge disappear out of the organisation and someone is always left needing to play catch up. It is a costly and foolhardy practice, ultimately. The everyday worker bees end up stuck and unable to progress, while witnessing director-level departures on 'fat cat' bonuses and pensions. It is very destabilising and creates depressed employees.

Also, due to the language and management challenges people end up avoiding decisions so that they do not get blamed for others' mistakes; more paralysis ensues.

Other security tasks for this month

Inventory management (yet again)

Users are now coming forward with all sorts of technology options that they use on a daily basis, and querying the security of these. So what about the use of headphones and privacy filter screens? Who should use these and what, if any, are the disability and accessibility issues versus the security issues they seek to resolve? The answers are whatever you decide they need to be for your organisation, your users and the nature of the information being used.

What about mobile devices with unencrypted onboard memory? These were mobile devices with only the SD cards encrypted, being used by mobile workers doing surveys. They needed to be advised to ensure that they closed out of the survey using the cross on the box or hit the refresh button to clear the contents. For each asset item, you can see the need to have it listed on the inventory, and to have some kind of reference column identifying the appropriate security control to secure the information that the asset is used to process, transfer or store.

As an aside on inventory management – watch out for the wily user. One most interesting help desk call we received was a claim for a new PC, using the 'excuse' that the PAT testing had failed on machine cables. Trying to get a whole new machine rather than just replacing the cables!

Ongoing laptop management issues

As a result of a decentralised purchasing process, it was not possible to control those devices that were out with the various departments, sections and teams. There was also a stockpile of laptops too old to put back into the estate. This was unfortunate, but proved to be a 'lessons-learnt' point in itself, particularly given the increasing attention being paid to laptop control by regulators and the media.

Homeworkers need to appreciate that if they have a laptop in their own home, no matter what they use it for, it will still be identifiable as belonging to a particular organisation if it has an asset tag, and it is that organisation that will end up in the news – even if the device is encrypted.

Port control

The background to the requirement to manage ports is well known by now. Under UK data protection legislation, data controllers have a responsibility to ensure that all reasonable steps are taken to mitigate the potential for data loss or breach of security. The seventh principle in the UK Data Protection Act requires an organisation, as data controller, to implement appropriate "technical and organisational" measures to keep personal data safe. Failure to do so exposes the organisation to the risk of fines, which can be up to £500,000. People constantly plug personal storage devices into their work PCs to upload music and wallpaper images, or transmit digital photos over the Internet. Their intent may be innocent. The capability to also siphon off corporate data from an endpoint, through a USB port on to a portable storage device, may place your organisation at considerable risk of undetected data leaks and exposure to malicious files. In this particular case, with the experience of the Conficker outbreak across the network, it turned out that the threat vector was considered to be unencrypted USB devices. Hence significant focus was needed on addressing this particular organisational vulnerability.

A standard corporate desktop PC may have up to eight USB ports. Some are required for peripherals, such as a keyboard or security token reader, but there are usually one or more unused ports. In the case of the organisation used as an example in this book USB ports are 'always on' by default, ready to serve any USB-enabled device that is plugged into the endpoint computer.

Your organisation may choose to disable USB access via the Windows® Group Policy and an Active Directory

Management (ADM) template, but this action does not provide administrators with granular control. It's all or nothing, so all USB ports on an endpoint are either available or not. And since most endpoints now require USB for mandatory peripherals, this control is practically useless. Solving this difficulty can require project team resources to investigate the best approach with regard to port control. However, cost may often dictate that a cheaper solution be deployed, even if it provides less security overall – and increases administrative overheads. This is just another of the many conundrums your role will involve you in, seeking to provide guidance and steering, and the best overall solution to meet all needs. It's a tall order and a difficult task.

Following a change in the political landscape and the resultant pull-back on spend, the intended port control project was stalled, so the control of removable media devices was not progressing as planned. A less expensive interim solution was being put in place using Active Directory to control ports. This highlighted an interesting difficulty with regard to tactics and approach. The accuracy of the data held within the Active Directory listing is always a vital starting point. Also, the Global Address List (GAL) is a fundamentally important element of your organisation's configuration and it is vital that you have accurate and up-to-date information contained therein. When it comes to users, it harks back to our references to the need to have an up-to-date user listing, so that you know who your user base is – and this can only be achieved and maintained with the assistance of the various teams that manage people in and out of the organisation. You also need to know who might require being on the 'exception' list, for whatever justified and risk-assessed reason, so that they can be excluded from any 'apply all' setting that is fixed in the Active Directory as a way to roll out a policy setting for all users.

In reality, so many of your tasks and challenges as an ISM will come back to this kind of conundrum – you cannot do anything effectively without quality information and a solid foundation upon which to move forward.

Outsourcing functions

When your staff are moving from your organisation to an umbrella third-party agency, can they really take their e-mail .pst files with them? If so, what level of review of these should take place, to ensure that your organisational information assets are not leaving inadvertently – particularly if the owner of the .pst was using it as a file repository system (records management store), as is mostly the reality. Just another of the myriad of conundrums you may face and which require answers appropriate for your organisation. If only it was possible to wave a magic wand and say that one answer fits all. The principles and the approach are the same, though. Consider the information assets at risk, the threat, the likelihood, the impact (on whom), etc. – and apply appropriate controls accordingly.

Security incident

An individual received 50 payslips in a brown envelope at their home address. They were on a short-term contract before going back to college and their own payslip was posted to their home, but obviously they were not expecting to receive the other 50 as well. It was obviously necessary to safely and securely get the payslips returned and appropriately distributed, and then reassure the individual that something like this would not happen again.

Security awareness theme

Being a Eurovision lover myself, my May theme usually builds up to something related to this European song festival! Given the multicultural world in which we live and the level of diversity we see all around us, this might work in your organisation, too. You could provide a national identity (United Nations style) for each department/ team/directorate and build in some level of competition between them in terms of the best clear-desk policy adherence group; the most secure (fewest incidents experienced) team at the end of the month; or the least frequent users of the help desk. Then remember to present some kind of 'award' at the end. A box of chocolates usually goes a long way!

Chapter summary

Another brief month, to reflect that there will be a level of ongoing day-to-day activities that arise and a level of repetitiveness - your journey towards embedding an optimised, information security-aware culture in the DNA of your organisation may be a long and potentially tortuous one. I'm just being honest!

You need to be a relentless beast to "Prove all things; hold fast that which is good" (1 Thessalonians 5:21).

CHAPTER 11: JUNE - WHAT THE AUDITORS SHOULDN'T KNOW...

Internal audit has history

The relationship with internal audit can often be fractious, but at the outset of this book, the intention was to portray information security in a positive light. Befriending internal audit is very much part of the experience, because you can so often find that any changes you need to implement have already been identified, long ago and many times over, in previous audit reports.

In the case of the organisation at the heart of many of these experiences, it had been subject to 'special measures' and was fraught with political infighting. This had a highly detrimental impact on the ability of the organisation to run effectively and efficiently. While it may feel that this is straying beyond the bounds of a typical ISM role, it is vital to understand the landscape within which you are forced to operate; particularly in a public sector role. You can then continue to make the necessary progress, in spite of all that is going on around you. There is always a 'bigger picture', an historical context and landscape to be considered and remembered while in the eddies of internal political wrangling.

The chronology in *Table 7* is designed to show how much history there can be in your organisation if you look for it - an understanding of the time line in which you are working can be most useful.

Table 7: Organisation's history

Date	Description	Comments
May 1997	Finance and general purposes subcommittee paper entitled 'Information technology – contingency planning and disaster recovery'.	"... planning to introduce best-practice notes during the course of 1997/1998 to aid departments to consider the issues involved." None have been specifically evidenced. Sadly, the hard copy available states "never sent" at the top.
Jun 1997	District audit network risk assessment sent to a senior manager. A strategic review was ongoing at the time – something the public sector suffers from a lot (14.5 years on and very little had changed, sadly).	Issues identified: • Lack of a defined and tested DR plan. • Lack of security, fault and performance management on the network. • Lack of standards, procedures and guidance for everyone to follow. ICT audit states that "activities of the risk assessment are a cause of concern".
Oct 1999	External risk management review of computer systems conducted.	Referenced issues with back-up, disaster recovery and implementation of risk management cases for all new systems.
Jun 2000	Qualified external auditor letter confirming the costs for assessment of the organisation against	Clearly the organisation had been considering certification to the then British Standard for Information Security Management Systems (BS7799 –

	BS7799:1999.	now an international standard, ISO27001).
Nov 2002	BS7799 registration project.	Over two years later, a BS7799 project initiation document (PID) was created. But nothing concrete appeared to happen to this project in the intervening years.
Nov 2002	Policies and principles manual includes information security.	Version 2, based on BS7799-2:2002 and following its structure in its entirety - but it was not implemented.
Nov 2002	Detailed application risk analysis.	Process and template prepared – not completed, embedded or shared.
Nov 2002	Homeworking detailed risk analysis v1.	Document completed, but there is no evidence that the actions were followed up.
2003	External information security course provision reviewed.	Presumably with a view to it being embedded and available within ICT and beyond – it included discussion/education about information classification.
Jun 2003	Data risk analysis v1.	ISM owner of risk management process – but it hasn't been used, completed or apparently shared.
Jun 2003	Detailed BS7799 action plan.	Document incomplete. If this had all been followed up and completed, the whole information security improvement programme and compliance efforts would have been a breeze – instant responses would have been available and the BS7799

		certification would have been evidence enough to pass external audit requirements.
Jun 2003	Information security action plan.	This covered all expected aspects including InfoSec policy and infrastructure, but personnel and InfoSec awareness sheets sadly were blank, empty of any tasks. The content relied heavily on resources provided by external consultancy services to assist in the completion of the tasks. Effort and expense was, therefore, in evidence as having been spent at the time.
Jul 2003	Asset inventory and risk assessment done.	A comprehensive risk analysis was carried out on the IT asset inventory – external consultancy support was utilised.
Aug 2003	Corporate business continuity planning introduced.	External support was offered to workshop with ICT to develop the appropriate service level BCP. BCP guidance notes were prepared (dated June 2003).
Feb 2005	Information assurance CD received from UK government technical authority provider.	This was part of an effort to extend advice given to central government to provide benefit to the wider public sector. The resource should have proved invaluable to the organisation as it contained policy documents and good practice guides (GPGs) which, if utilised and implemented, would have provided an appropriate

		framework of security control across information assets.
Oct 2005	Second edition of Information Assurance Guidance for the Wider Public Sector CD received from UK government technical authority provider.	This CD includes IS2 – a tool providing policy and guidance on the risk management and accreditation of information systems. Again, the aim in providing this resource was to ensure that organisations were aware of security and connectivity requirements and expectations.
Feb 2007	ISO27001 audit report (internal).	An audit was carried out in Dec 2006, reflecting that in 2004 significant progress needed to be made and a previous audit was, thus, abandoned. So the work commenced in 2003 clearly went nowhere, sadly, and in reality no progress has been made since. It was disappointing to read the audit report stating that progress and likelihood of achieving the standard was 'adequate', when a current, up-to-date copy of the standard was not available at the time.
Apr 2008	Letter to all chief executives from an external third-party secure network provider.	This was signed by all the relevant connectivity strategic partners – requesting that chief executives champion their authorities' early adoption of the intended new secure network.
Apr 08	Secure network provider letter.	The secure network became a cross-government programme. The connectivity was described as being a "key strategic enabler to

		improving public services for citizens and communities".
Jun 2008	Audit of ICT network security – action plan.	A senior ICT manager made a commitment that security roles were to be clarified through job descriptions in the intended new structure – with a target date of December 2008. At this time, another key audit recommendation was to embed the following. "A policy on the connection of non-standard equipment to the network should be determined following an investigation into the feasibility of a cost-effective method of locking out any non-approved equipment being undertaken." However, this was rejected due to the potential user disruption and amount of work likely to be generated as a result.
Jul 2008	Another letter from the secure network consortium to all senior information risk owners.	This letter advised the organisation of important revisions to the data access policy. However, without a key ISM in post, it was clear that such communication was not being appropriately handled as no one really knew what to do with it.
Jul 2008	Communication from the external consortium and its government sponsor.	A direct request from the government was made to the organisation, requesting it to place an order for connection to the secure network.

Aug 2008	Third-party consortium letter to all senior information risk owners.	This letter provided details of the exemption process for those not opting for early connection to the secure network. Sadly, the public sector way is rarely an early adopter, in spite of the writing obviously being on the wall. The reality is usually that the longer the wait, the more expensive the implementation, as your technology and security has been left to fall behind in the intervening period of time.
Sep 2008	Senior executive management decision-making meeting.	Agenda item – senior ICT managers briefed service reps on the secure network and what was involved to gain connectivity.
Sep 2008	Business case submitted.	The BC outlined the 92 requirements.
Sep 2008	Letter from the organisation's senior information risk owner to the government.	Requesting an exemption from the data access policy until 30/09/09. This then left two weeks to produce a 'code of connection' submission return to the government, explaining what the organisation was doing to meet the 92 requirements.
Oct 2008	Third-party consortium letter to senior information risk owner.	The exemption request was approved.
Nov 2008	Government department letter to local department	This was a 'memorandum of understanding' of what to expect during the transition of operational processing to secure

	section.	connectivity.
Dec 2008	Third-party consortium letter to senior information risk owners.	Advising of file transfer arrangements, which in reality did not seem entirely secure.
Dec 2008	Externally available article on remote working.	It was clear that secure connectivity mandated controls that precluded remote workers from using their own PCs at home, even when using a secure virtual desktop, thus requiring the organisation to supply all remote and homeworking staff with organisation-controlled equipment. This was an added expense and management overhead.
Jan 2009	Another government department set of guidance notes was produced and circulated.	This did not arrive with the right people within the organisation until November 2009 – at which point there were only two months left before their insecure connectivity was turned off in January 2010. This was another example of a clear lack of understanding of the importance of the various missives coming out of central government relating to networks, security and connectivity. The lack of an appropriately appointed ISM meant the organisation risked being unable to fulfil its obligations with regard to service delivery while maintaining the security of its information assets.

Feb 2009	Land registry full network access agreement produced.	As with the above, this arrived in the right place in November 2009 – with the old service to be turned off from January 2010. Shorter timescales to implement the required secure network connectivity risked mistakes by the project team – never a position an ISM wants to find themselves in.
Feb 2009	More guidance issued from a government department regarding one of the corporate systems.	The ISM first heard about this on 15 December 2009, with a lead time of two weeks to implement by the deadline of 28 December 2009.
Apr 2009	External request for further connectivity.	Another external requirement appeared that required a different service area to utilise a secure connection. This took another nine months to filter its way through to the ISM to be dealt with properly.
Jun 2009	A project team was finally pulled together internally.	First meeting took place where the data access policy was discussed and the implications of the work ahead to deliver the project were appreciated.
Jun 2009	Business case submitted.	Revised BC was presented to senior management requesting funding. Finally, the penny drops, resources are made available and a project is instigated that has to operate under stressful conditions due to the tight timescales afforded.

What is depicted in *Table 7* is largely replicated across many organisations and should resonate with many readers. It is not uncommon for there to be many (often failed) attempts at getting proper information security procedures off the ground. Refer back to the opening statement of this book – information security is *not* a project ... and there's the rub. As long as it is tackled in your organisation as such, there is the risk of a disaster. It must be accepted as part of the fabric of the organisation. Information security management is as much a vital component as financial and people management. What the auditors know is vital in helping to tell the story to sell this message across the organisation.

However, when there is a significant audit finding that is made known to the appropriate governance group, and the choice made is to 'bury the bad news', this can present the ISM with an ethical dilemma.

A laptop audit was conducted that identified results that were considered to be 'too explosive'. After all the work that had been done on the desktop infrastructure, and after months of trying to gain some traction on the laptop estate, audit finally made an attempt to apply some metrics and measurement to this vital area. It was hard to explain away the fact that the organisation could have 1,500 laptops on its hardware asset inventory log and yet only 300 laptops connected to the network for updates, especially at a time when similar organisations were being fined for not being able to evidence appropriate controls across their 'estate' to protect information in all its guises and in all its states.

That was until I came across an organisation that knew it had over 300,000 laptops of which:

- 220,000 were encrypted;

- 70,000 were unaccounted for;
- 10,000 were 'waivered' – i.e. allowed to be outside the expected security policy process.

The number outside the scope of security policy requirements was significant and could not be explained away. Obviously, all things are relative and there are always issues with reporting and statistics that make a fool of those reporting them, which does none of us any favours. But this situation was made worse by the decision not to present the findings to the corporate management team for their view and guidance. There was a corporate annual audit taking place the following month and, unfortunately, there were tactics and politics at work. This meant that the decision taken was to maintain the laptop audit report as a 'confidential draft' for the subsequent few months, during which it would be possible to create an action plan that would evidence solutions to make the reading ultimately more palatable. Audit reports are not necessarily designed to be 'palatable'. They are supposed to represent the facts of any situation at the time, as found, and are intended to signpost areas of action required with recommendations for appropriate routes forward.

Remember your memberships – professional bodies have resources to help you through just these kinds of scenario, so don't be afraid to reach out, in confidence.

As previously advised, work closely with internal (and external) audit, and make sure you can help them in formulating an annual audit plan to cover the areas of highest priority when reflected across threat, vulnerability, risk assessment and business impact, etc.

Increasing and varied security incidents

As a result of having put in an appropriate information security incident reporting process, more information was now being provided to management and the perception was that information security incidents were increasing. This was obviously not the message that needed to be conveyed at a time when money was being spent on improving security! However, this is the risk of opening up the organisation and encouraging honesty about the real state of security. It is definitely a case of 'it usually gets worse before it gets better'. Once you shine the light on a situation, you see it 'warts and all' and this gives you the opportunity to embed more appropriate solutions for the future to help reduce this apparent volume of incidents.

The incidents were being reported mainly because, by now, people were ringing up with their woes, as they realised that what had hitherto been their normal practice was probably unwise. An individual called, concerned that they had no keys for their cabinets, but that their work pattern required them to often leave their desk in a hurry, leaving papers out and visible all the time. The easy solution was for them to get into the habit of putting their papers in a drawer, at least.

Laptop incidents

It transpired that a laptop provided to the organisation by external funding was obviously not needed as it was never networked and never used. The individual it was intended for used her husband's laptop instead, as he also worked for the organisation. What would you do? For transparency, you are supposed to be able to evidence where the money went and what you did with it – obviously. But, given your programme of improvement, what you really want to do is to health-check and update the laptop, and ensure it goes to a user that needs it instead. In straitened times, there is nothing worse than having unused resources.

Some users had laptops, but were told they were not allowed to remove them from the building. However, since they were not needed inside the building, as everyone had desktops to use, they had not been on the intranet for ages and password lock-out had occurred. This was a useless situation for everyone. But it helped to highlight a cultural issue; people had the perception that 'it's my laptop', rather than 'it's an organisational asset'. With the latter attitude, appropriate reallocation is a lot easier!

Another user never connected their laptop to the network as they only used it at home. They transferred data to an encrypted USB from their work PC and then worked on the laptop at home. Obviously, they did not realise that this rendered the laptop potentially exposed, as it was never having its antivirus updated or patches applied.

One particular team was taking photos of what they did and putting them on a laptop, which was neither password protected nor kept in a locked cupboard.

One user was transferring 16,000 records on a laptop to CDs when they were all stolen, laptop and CDs, from the user's house. This was equivalent to a similar incident by an equivalent organisation that received a significant fine by the regulator, but in this case the user was contracted by an independent third-party provider. Who takes the hit?

Spreadsheets and attachments

Many teams still use spreadsheet and Word attachments in e-mails, as opposed to inputting data into the available corporate systems. Thus, there is a risk of data loss as these e-mails fly around, both inside the safe and secure corporate system and outside it. This is happening every day in most organisations, but it doesn't mean that the underlying issues don't need to be resolved. People need to be encouraged to share hyperlinks, rather than e-mailing attachments. Part of the larger task is keeping some kind of time line for the number of available corporate systems and their level of usage, compared to the level of sensitivity of the information contained therein. If data is being 'lifted' out in order to put it into a more usable format to suit the user, this is causing greater risk - therefore, data loss prevention mechanisms need to be considered.

Postal failures

An original agreement was sent to the wrong person, in the wrong organisation. They were asked to send it back by post, but it went missing. Now, what do you do? To whom should the breach be reported, if at all? These small incidents are occurring all the time and your radar needs to be alive to them. Depending on the prevailing circumstances you will be able to come up with an appropriate solution, but be prepared to be a focus for those concerned as they try and work through their own panic at being caught like a bunny in the headlights.

And yet a postal guide was produced that made no reference to protective marking or handling of volume data. Again, this is a classic example of people thinking only in a silo, isolated from understanding the need to engage the ISM in all cases of activity relating to information assets – usually the change can only begin when people accept and understand what an information asset is.

Printing problems

Printer servers were not set up properly as file and print servers and old printers were not properly removed or decommissioned. This is another one of those 'things to remember', as it can cause havoc for users when selecting default printers and trying to maintain their usual work patterns and productivity.

Removable media management

Mixed communication messages were being received across departments. One team was told that their department could not afford encrypted USB sticks, so they resorted to buying them from a shop. Other users were backing up data on to a portable hard drive purchased similarly, which was also not encrypted. The portable hard drive was being taken home and the data then used for remote working. If, at any point, it had been lost or stolen, this would have been an embarrassing data breach for the organisation. The larger your organisation is, the harder it is to get the right message to everyone at the same time, unless you have a mandate to do so. But these kinds of incident really illustrate the need to get permission to send the message as quickly as is humanly possible.

> Incidents and frustrations are arising everywhere. A third-party integration provider spent two years trying to get a server to be switched off because it was allowing spam through its appropriate protection software. The software could see it, but the server was erroneously configured, out of date and out of band. Sadly, committee meeting after committee meeting took place with no progress being made. All the while, the organisation was at risk.

Access control issues

There were users in the organisation with full system access through remote connectivity and, therefore, the ability to copy everything to their home PCs. At times like this, your natural instinct is to despair! The ability to retain and maintain control can be extremely limited, given what the regulators expect, if we are honest.

Password management anomalies

Passwords appeared visible, in the clear, when logging into the organisation intranet and the 90-day password reset was not working. The users had been so well prepared for the full password reset roll-out that they were had heightened awareness of these kinds of anomalies, which arose as a result of outlying departments not always being captured by system changes. This was definitely something for the ISM to keep putting pressure on IT colleagues to keep abreast of.

Physical security conundrums

An individual attended a security awareness briefing then went back to their desk, left their phone plugged in and charging, their wallet on the desk, and dashed out. They came back for their keys, but still left all these other personal belongings. Oh, the irony!

(ISM solution – have a toolkit, in which you have available, amongst many other things, a set of postcards that you can use to leave on people's desks when they do silly things like this!)

In this particular case, the team were working in a building where the doors were not locked until 6:30 pm. People closed the blinds, but left keys in the cabinets and in the key cabinet, and a lot of paperwork and items on desks. There were also roller cabinets that could not be locked.

Guests were not chaperoned out after meetings, and yet it was possible to walk past a number of unlocked screens and see organisational and citizen-sensitive information on display.

These kinds of things can be reported back in the same way as our findings in *Chapter 2*.

All of this is going on, and yet there are still people who believe that information security is not relevant to them, or that it does not warrant a full-time employee in the role!

Security awareness theme

Start considering messages around a holiday theme. Users go away for their two-week break from June onwards and they return revived and refreshed, but having wiped their mind clean of all things to do with work. They've 'lost' the synapse that contains their password, too! If the 90-day password reset occurs while they are away, and they miss it, that's even worse! Remember to prepare your help desk for an increase in reset calls in the coming months, too.

Chapter summary

This chapter focused on two particular areas that, put together, provide a time line of understanding for how things come unstuck. Internal and external audit reports will always be available in any organisation. These are a gold-dust resource for the ISM to trawl through and see what the recurring themes have been over time, and whether improvements have been embedded. If not, research the barriers and help come up with workable solutions through the security improvement programme.

It is appreciated that it may just be, sadly, that the culture of the organisation will render it ultimately impossible to achieve sweeping change, but 'slowly, slowly, catchy monkey', as one particular saying goes. It is still possible to make some change and achieve improved information security from the bottom up, if doing so from the top down is proving unsuccessful.

CHAPTER 12: JULY - JOURNEY'S END... AND CONCLUSION

Returning to the lessons learnt

When your pet project gets cancelled, how do you move forward? Therein lies the rub of labelling anything in the information security space as a 'project'. As we have seen throughout this book, it needs to be incorporated into the DNA of the organisational infrastructure and so there is no ending, as it is constantly changing and adapting to the threat and vulnerability landscape within which we are operating.

Equally, as an ISM, you need to know the business. The IT community in its entirety is so often charged with 'not understanding the business', so as a professional (see section below) it is important that you take the time to learn as much as you can about your environment – as we saw and learnt in *Chapter 1*. This is most often referred to as 'situational awareness' and requires constant vigilance, in particular, to assimilate the nuances of both the culture and the language being used by those around you, so that you can seek to mirror it. The more you can successfully achieve this, the better your results will be when you are trying to either change behaviour or gain support for a change in activity – any change which is designed to provide greater security and protection for both the individuals to whom the change will apply and the individuals whose information may be tangentially involved, too.

12: July - Journey's end ... and conclusion

The life of an information security manager

So what have we learnt about being an ISM?

You should never be idle or bored, that's for sure! It is possible to try to apply some level of structure across your year, if you are not experiencing too much organisational flux or change. There are constantly recurring themes – laptop management, password management, access control, server management, etc. This is to be expected. Things reoccur which would disappear once dealt with, but which, if you just stick on a plaster, will keep on coming back. Your role is very much one of providing solutions, often in difficult circumstances, so think creatively, too.

It's an 'always on' existence, as you are always considering the dangers that may arise. The more you allow this kind of thinking to become second nature, the more you can apply the solutions you come up with to your day-to-day role.

How long does it take for something to become an established discipline, understood and followed by all? What is the motivation for adoption? Will mandating make this adoption more successful? Your user base will, in some cases, have a 'what's in it for me?' mentality and you must be sure to address it. We have seen that there will be challenges around compliance: personalities, prioritisation, internal versus external politics, convergence, centralisation and professionalism. Ultimately, you will need collaboration to gain trust – across teams and across the whole organisation. You need to be a counsellor, guide and adviser, busy all the time working out ways to inspire and enthuse those around you!

In the preface, I described the reality; that so many people find themselves in the role of ISM after having it presented to them as a 'gift'. So, often, you are left feeling like you have received a poisoned chalice. It is a constant uphill battle trying to persuade people to do different things.

Imagine, if you will, that you are in the care of the dental hygienist. Over the years, the dental practice has found that they can reduce time spent in the dentist's chair by increasing the time spent in the dental hygienist's chair, instead. It's not clear that this is any more pleasant for anyone, but the idea is that they are moving from a reactive to a more preventative approach. So the dental hygienist will tell you, on each and every occasion that you visit, that you need to floss more, you need to use the interdental brushes and you need to work your main brush into the gaps between your teeth to reduce plaque and ultimately reduce tooth decay and gum disease. You can end up feeling both patronised and chastised by this, in equal measure, depending on your behaviour. It comes down to the choices you have made in the intervening time.

Delivering robust information security into and across your organisation can be considered in alignment with this thinking. What you are trying to do is implement controls that will be prove to be preventative and will reduce the need for fire-fighting. They will protect the information assets of all concerned (the teeth) if suitably constructed and enforced.

As the ISM, there will be a time when you will need to take on battles with the organisation itself, effectively holding up the mirror of sense in the face of seemingly nonsensical and conflicting requirements. If you spot inconsistencies with regard to the planned roll-out of systems, find a way to communicate this. This is not a role for a wallflower.

Things I haven't spent a lot of time on

These include other frameworks (e.g. COBIT®), regulatory requirements (e.g. the PCI DSS), standards (e.g. ISO27001) and activities, such as undertaking back-up, risk assessments and business continuity planning. Some of these activities could be done in February, as it seems to be a quiet month! There are many great resources to address all of these issues directly. There will no doubt be other things, too, that you might think I should have spent some time on. I hope that this goes to illustrate quite how much there is to be done in the role of ISM. I may not have focused on everything, but it all needs to be done!

In many ways, we have only scratched the surface. There's a long career available to you if you take up the challenge of being chief protector of all things information in your organisation! Or, at least caring enough to try and grab attention from as wide an audience as possible across your organisation.

Closing thoughts

What this book was designed to do was take the reader on a journey through a year in the life of an ISM. This has been delivered in a combination of real time and the past tense, and I hope the reader will forgive that as it is only from reflecting on the past that we can learn lessons for the present and adapt the learning for the future.

There may be no particular 'eureka' moments, but it is hoped that putting together these thoughts and experiences in one place for reference will provide a level of sanity checking that will prove helpful in ensuring you get the best out of your day-to-day interactions in the role of ISM. You are an important company asset.

Some thoughts to help consolidate key learning points:

- Don't constrain yourself to technological concerns. Think more broadly.
- Have a mission and do all that you can to stick to it. For example, 'Information is at the heart of all that we do, and we will all endeavour to protect it accordingly.'

I hope that you have seen enough to be sure that it's a full-time job and to be confident in explaining to your management why it should be kept as such and resourced appropriately.

And finally, be an active professional

There is a lot of work going on in the industry to professionalise IA in particular. Certifications are already available for information security professionals. This all holds tremendous value and you should either be involved in development from the ground up, or ensure that you are maintaining your own continuous professional development. For example, as a result of reading this book, it may be that you need to focus on information and RM learning.

Read old internal audit reports – and obviously new ones, too!

Be a member of the relevant bodies, for example:

- ISACA – *www.isaca.org.uk/*
- ISSA – *https://issa.org/*
- ISSP – www.iisp.org/

- BCS – *www.bcs.org/*
- IAPP – *www.privacyassociation.org/*
- AIIM – *www.aiim.org/*
- DP Forum (in the UK) – *www.dpforum.org.uk/*
- BCI – *www.thebci.org/*
- IRMS – *www.irms.org.uk/*.

Read the monthly journals from these various professional bodies and membership groups. Also, follow up on references and resources from articles in the journals and reach out to their authors. Most authors welcome feedback and communication, and you can build a wider network of like-minded people with whom to touch base, who will be able to assist you when you need help.

The bottom line has to be – read voraciously! There is a lot to keep up to date with, so you need to do your best to stay on top of the constant march of progress in the information industry. Rest assured, there is every chance we will swing back around through the Cloud and virtualisation journey to a more mainframe-like existence, in the coming years. This will be a bumpy journey, no doubt, alongside which will be the need to manage a growing level of externally hosted information assets through a vast array of technology. There will be a growing integration of devices and services – smartphones synchronised with home PCs and TVs. The role of the ISM will not get any easier, or any less important, as these advances will all make it harder for organisations to know where their information has gone, even if the user is still working for them. And, of course, the situation produces a very large attack surface.

Keep your security radar up and your knowledge level as high as you possibly can – and never lose your sense of humour!

APPENDIX 1: SECURITY AWARENESS THEMES

Each month, consider focusing on a subject suitable for the time of the year and harnessing your information security endeavours to that. It helps to keep the subject at the forefront of everyone's considerations and ensures that you are incorporating information security into the DNA of your organisation, embedding it into best practice and slowly, but surely, changing the culture for the better.

Always use whatever news stories have appeared during the month. There is no shortage of these, day in and day out, that should be crossing your desk as the ISM, but they may not even register for the average user. In fact, there are many stories that appear in the news that involve information security but are not deliberately presented in this light by the media. But you can find the security element – be it a personnel issue, a physical security issue, a technical security issue or an information-specific security issue. Let your creative juices flow!

However trite these suggestions may seem, the user population will have some appreciation for the mix of irony and humour and at least will see that there is a theme and a messaging effort going on.

Security awareness theme – January

This month's information security theme could pick up on the fact that January is usually a time for New Year's resolutions. For example, 'So what's yours …? Ours is to always update our antivirus …' or 'New Year, New attitude … let's lock down those devices!'

Appendix 1: Security Awareness Themes

Security awareness theme – February

This month's information security theme could pick up on the fact that the media focus is usually, at least for the first two weeks of February, related to Valentine's Day, so there's a 'love' element. You could run a campaign entitled 'Love your Laptop', where users are encouraged to ensure that they have connected to the network, updated the patches and antivirus status, run a back-up, cleaned out the cookies and Internet history, etc.

Security awareness theme – March

This month's information security theme could pick up on any subject of your choice. In this particular example and experience from the chapter, tackling antivirus best practice would be the obvious choice! As long as you encourage the users to ensure that they update their own antivirus product on their home machines, they will appreciate the scale of the effort you will be applying across your whole organisation when it comes to protection mechanisms.

Security awareness theme – April

This month's information security theme should usually be focusing on Easter, as it arises at this time. You could run a campaign whereby you leave chocolates (mini eggs, for example, to keep in theme!) on the desks of those users who are adhering to your clear-desk policy.

Security awareness theme – May

Being a Eurovision lover myself, my May theme usually builds up to something related to this European song festival! Given the multicultural world in which we live and the level of diversity we see all around us, this might work in your organisation, too. You could provide a national identity (United Nations style) for each department/team/ directorate and build in some level of competition between them in terms of the best clear-desk policy adherence group; the most secure (fewest incidents experienced) team at the end of the month; or the least frequent users of the help desk. Then remember to present some kind of 'award' at the end. A box of chocolates usually goes a long way!

Security awareness theme – June

Start considering messaging around a holiday theme. Users go away for their two-week break from June onwards and they return revived and refreshed, but having wiped their mind clean of all things to do with work. They've 'lost' the synapse that contains their password, too. If the 90-day password reset occurs while they are away, and they miss it, that's even worse! Remember to prepare your help desk for an increase in reset calls in the coming months, too.

Security awareness theme – July

Summer months will be an ideal time to focus on removable media device (RMD) security. There is a great concern, with the number of people commuting and travelling and the increased numbers of people in general, that there will be a resultant increase in loss of removable media devices. Make sure your message theme shares best practice on securing all devices when away from the usual workplace.

Security awareness theme – August

Follow up your July theme on RMD with a message theme on home/remote working itself, from airports (and using wireless networks) to hotels. Combine this with encouraging a heightened awareness of physical security issues too, relevant to your user base and their information assets.

Security awareness theme – October

This month's information security theme could pick up on the fact October ends with Halloween, a yearly holiday celebrated around the world. Given the volume of malware, spyware and spooky tales to tell in the world of security, there's enough to hang your ISM hat on, if you are creative enough!

Security awareness theme – November

This month's information security theme could pick up on the fact that November contains Bonfire Night, very quickly after Halloween. Utilising the 'Remember, remember the fifth of November' mantra, you can play on that and deliver messages around 'Remember, remember… your removable media devices!' or 'Remember, remember… to clear your desk before you leave every day!' Or take it up a notch and go for a fireworks-related theme.

Security awareness theme – December

This month's information security theme should definitely pick up on Christmas – focusing on the aspect of gift-giving so as not to cause any religious offence. Picking up on the well-used phrase 'A dog is for life, not just for Christmas' you could pick any element of best-practice information security and the same would apply. 'Back-up is for life, not just for Christmas' perhaps?

APPENDIX 2: ISM ACTIVITIES

There are many activities or tasks that an ISM has to contend with and they obviously can't all be done in one month. You need to try and spread your activity across the year with some level of planning, so that you are not constantly fire-fighting. Below are the key headlines from each of the chapters, represented as task points for an ISM to focus on.

ISM activities – January

- Embedding security culture
- Desktop refresh and consumerisation
- Incident reporting
- Data-sharing protocols/information sharing agreements
- Records management
- Penetration testing
- Environmental management issues

ISM activities – February

- User administration (and rights management)
- Inventory management
- Review back-up arrangements
- Review business continuity requirements and engage widely across the business, conducting business impact analyses
- Review risk assessment arrangements across the whole organisation

Appendix 2: ISM Activities

ISM activities – March

- Addressing user requirements
- Privacy impact assessments
- Managing a virus outbreak
- Embedding a useful InfoSec intranet

ISM activities – April

- Reviewing information assurance arrangements
- Linking up with information governance requirements
- Security metrics and measurements
- Equipment life-cycle management

ISM activities – May

- Maintaining situational awareness
- Addressing language and management challenges
- Laptop management
- Outsourcing/third-party management
- Addressing port control

ISM activities – June

- Reviewing audit reports – internal and external
- Review other project proposals
- Review organisational complaints
- Security incident response management
- Access control
- Removable media device management

ISM activities – July

- Reading – journal articles, books, blogs

- Maintaining continuous professional development

ISM activities – August

- Identify all assets – hardware, software, information, people
- People – network widely
- Review access control
- Review information security awareness levels and design new material
- Review incident management processes and improve if necessary

ISM activities – September

- Software licensing
- Remote and mobile worker management
- User acceptance testing
- Addressing physical security (convergence)
- Password management
- Laptop management

ISM activities – October

- Information security policy creation and development
- Antivirus (malware) management
- Standard build and image roll-out
- Password management (again)
- Audit log management
- Vulnerability management
- Cloud Computing – third-party management, etc.
- Project and people management

ISM activities – November

- Remote working (again) – location network set-up
- Ensuring security is built into *all* projects from the outset
- Information labelling and classification of information assets
- Ensuring lessons learnt are recorded and shared

ISM activities – December

- Security improvement programme (SIP)
- Fax management
- Image build (again)
- Physical security (again)

APPENDIX 3: RESOURCES

Reference books and articles

Boyce JG and Jennings DW, (2002), *Information Assurance: Managing Organizational IT Security Risks*, Butterworth Heinemann, London, ISBN 0-7506-7527-3. (This article was published in Information Assurance: Managing Organizational IT Security Risks, pp.170–171, copyright Butterworth Heinemann (2002).)

British Standards Institution, (2009), *ISO 31000: 2009, Risk Management Principles and Guidance Standard*, London.

Dimitriadis CK, (2011), Information Security from a Business Perspective, *ISACA Journal*, vol. 1. [Accessed 18 February 2011.] Available at: *www.continuitycentral.com/feature0856.html*.

Herrmann DS, (2002), *A practical guide to Security Engineering and Information Assurance*, Auerbach Publications, CRC Press, Florida, ISBN 0-8493-1163-2.

Hutton N, (2008), Information Assurance: 'Must try harder', *ITAdviser*, Winter, pp.16–17. [Accessed 7 February 2011.] Available at: *www.360is.com/downloads/ncc-mag-issue-56-360is.pdf*.

Information Assurance Advisory Council (IAAC), (2003), Engaging the Board – Corporate Governance and Information Assurance, Board Report, February 2003, *www.iaac.org.uk*.

ISACA, (2009), An Introduction to the Business Model for Information Security, p.13, Figure 2, Overview of BMIS, ISACA, Illinois. [Accessed 20 March 2011.] Available at:

www.isaca.org/bmis, www.isaca.org/Knowledge-Center/BMIS/Pages/Business-Model-for-Information-Security.aspx, © 2010, ISACA. ® All rights reserved.

Kovacich GL, (1998), *Information Systems Security Officer's Guide, Establishing and Managing an Information Protection Program*, Butterworth Heinemann, Woburn, ISBN 0-7506-9896-9.

Maconachy V, Schou C, Ragsdale D and Welch D, (2001), *A Model for Information Assurance: An Integrated Approach*, Proceedings of the 2001 IEEE Workshop on Information Assurance and Security, June, U.S. Military Academy. West Point, New York, ISBN 0-7803-9814-9. [Accessed 8 July 2012.] Available at *http://darpa.academia.edu/DanielRagsdale/Papers/762175/A_model_for_information_assurance_An_integrated_appr oach*.

Marks N, (2011), Marks on Governance Blog – Podcast on GRC and a Related Discussion Forum, posted on 21 February 2011. [Accessed 27 February 2011.] Available at: *www.theiia.org/blogs/marks/index.cfm/post/Norman's%20 Podcast%20on%20GRC,%20and%20a%20Related%20Dis cussion%20Forum*.

McCumber J, (1991), Information Systems Security: A Comprehensible Model. Paper presented at the Proceedings of 14th National Computer Security Conference, National Institute of Standards and Technology, Baltimore, MD, October. Contains the McCumber Cube. [Accessed 3 February 2011.]

McCumber J, (2004), *Assessing and Managing Security Risk in IT Systems: A Structured Methodology*, Auerbach Publications, Florida, ISBN 0-8493-2232-4.

McFadzean E, (2005), The case for Information Assurance and Corporate Strategy Alignment, Part 5, Henley Management College, provided via *www.bl.uk* ref 9350.837405.

Open Compliance and Ethics Group (OCEG), (2011), Governance Risk and Compliance [GRC]. [Accessed 27 February 2011.] Available at: *www.oceg.org*.

OSI Model, Wikipedia Commons, *http://en.wikipedia.org/wiki/File:Osi-model.png*. [Accessed 8 July 2012.]

Petersen R, Larsen R, Schou C and Strickland L, (2004), What's in a name? *EDUCAUSE Quarterly*, vol. 27, no. 3, p.5–8. [Accessed 13 May 2010.] Available at: *www.educause.edu/EDUCAUSE+Quarterly/EDUCAUSEQ uarterlyMagazineVolum/WhatsinaName/157298*.

Schneier B, (2008), *Schneier on Security*, Wiley Publishing, Canada, ISBN 978-0-470-39535-6.

Shostack A and Stewart A, (2008), *New School of Information Security*, Addison Wesley, Boston, ISBN-13: 978-0-321-508728-0.

Schou C and Shoemaker D, (2007), *Information Assurance for the Enterprise: A Roadmap to Information Security,* McGraw-Hill Irwin, New York, ISBN-10: 0-07-225524-2/ ISBN-13: 978-0-07-225524-9.

Stoneburner G, (2001), Underlying Technical Models for Information Technology Security, NIST SP 800-33, US National Institute of Standards and Technology (NIST), December. [Accessed 6 February 2011.] Available at: *http://csrc.nist.gov/publications/nistpubs/800-33/sp800-33.pdf*.

UK CESG, (undated), Certification, Cheltenham. [Accessed 20 March 2011.] Available at: *www.cesg.gov.uk/publications/Documents/cccert.pdf*.

UK CESG, (undated), Protection Profiles, Cheltenham. [Accessed 20 March 2011.] Available at: *www.cesg.gov.uk/publications/Documents/criteria.pdf*.

US Department of the Air Force, (2001) AFI33-204, Information Assurance Awareness Program, September. [Accessed 2 February 2011.] Available at: *www.dtic.mil/cgi-bin/GetTRDoc?Location=U2&doc=GetTRDoc.pdf&AD=ADA405017*.

Wylder J, (2004), *Strategic Information Security,* CRC/ Auerbach Publications, Florida, ISBN 0-8493-2041-0.*www.dtic.mil/cgi-bin/GetTRDoc?Location=U2&doc=GetTRDoc.pdf&AD=ADA405017*

Further resources

It is hoped that the following list of further resources will be useful to the reader wishing to embark on wider research of the topics discussed within this report.

Alexander D, Finch A and Sutton D, (2008), *Information Security Management Principles, An ISEB Certificate*, Andy Taylor (ed.), BCS Books, ISBN-13: 978-1-902505-90-9.

BSI Business Information Publishing, (2008), *Exercising for Excellence, Delivering Successful Business Continuity Management Exercises*, Crisis Solutions, (BIP 2143) ISBN-13: 978-0-580-50953-7.

Calder A (2005), *The Case for ISO27001*, IT Governance Publishing, ISBN-10: 1-905356-13-7.

Calder A, (2005), *Nine Steps to Success, An ISO27001 Implementation Overview*, IT Governance Publishing, ISBN-10: 1-905356-12-9.

Day K, (2003), *Inside the Security Mind – Making the Tough Decisions*, Prentice Hall, ISBN-10: 0-13-111829-3.

Denning DE, (2000), *Information Warfare and Security*, ACM Press, ISBN-10: 0-201-43303-6.

Desman MB, (2002), *Building an Information Security Awareness Program*, CRC/Auerbach Publications, Florida, ISBN 0-8493-0116-5.

Greene TC, (2004), *Computer Security for the Home and Small Office*, _www.apress.com_, ISBN-10: 1-590593-16-2.

Hare-Brown N, (2007), *Information Security Incident Management – A Methodology*, BSI Business Information Publishing, ISBN-13: 978-0-580-50720-5.

Holt J and Newton J (eds), (2004), *A Manager's Guide to IT Law*, BCS Books, ISBN-10: 1-902505-55-7.

Institute of Internal Auditors, (2010), A Culture of Risk, *Tone at the Top*, Issue 46, February, Florida.

John Wylder, (2004), *Strategic Information Security*, Auerbach, ISBN-10: 0-8493-2041-0.

Jones A and Ashenden D, (2005), *Risk Management for Computer Security, Protecting Your Network and Information Assets*, Elsevier, ISBN-10: 0-75-6-7795-3.

Lierley M (compilation ed.), (2001), *Security Complete*, Sybex Inc, ISBN-10: 0-7821-2968-4.

Mitnick K and Simon WL, (2002), *The Art of Deception*, Wiley: *www.wiley.com*, ISBN-10: 0-7645-4280-X.

Moses R and Archer H, (2006), *Delivering and Managing Real-World Network Security*, BSI Business Information Publishing, ISBN 0-580-48985.

Nichols RK, Ryan DJ and Ryan JJCH, (2000), *Defending Your Digital Assets*, RSA Press, ISBN-10: 0-07-213024-5.

O'Hara K and Shadbolt N, (2008), *The Spy in the Coffee Machine*, Oneworld, Oxford, ISBN-13: 978-1-85168-554-7.

Oppliger R, (1998), *Internet and Intranet Security*, Artech House Publishers, ISBN-10: 0-89006-829-1.

Parker DB, (2010), Our Excessively Simplistic Information Security Model and How to Fix It, *ISSA Journal*, July.

Peltier TR, (2001), *Information Security Risk Analysis*, CRC/Auerbach Publications, Florida, ISBN 0-8493-0880-1.

Peltier TR, (2002), *Information Security Policies, Procedures, and Standards, Guidelines for Effective Information Security Management*, CRC/Auerbach Publications, Florida, ISBN 0-8493-1137-3.

Peltier TR, (2004), *Information Security Policies and Procedures, A Practitioner's Reference*, Second Edition, CRC/Auerbach Publications, Florida, ISBN 0-8493-1958-7.

POA Publishing LLC, (2003), *Asset Protection and Security Management Handbook*, Auerbach Publishing, ISBN 0-8493-1603-0.

Rothke B, (2004), *Computer Security, 20 Things Every Employee Should Know*, McGraw-Hill, ISBN-10: 0-07-223083-5.

Schneier B, (2000), *Secrets and Lies: Digital Security in a Networked World*, John Wiley & Sons, New York, ISBN 0-471-25311-1.

Schneier B, (2003), *Beyond Fear, Thinking Sensibly About Security in an Uncertain World*, Copernicus Books, New York, ISBN 0-387-02620-7.

Schou CD, Trimmer CD and Trimmer KJ, (2004), Information Assurance and Security, Idaho State University, *Journal of Organizational and End User Computing*, Vol. 16, No. 3, pp.1.

Schwartau W, (1994), *Information Warfare*, Thunder's Mouth Press, ISBN-10: 1-56025-132-8.

Sharp J, (2007), *The Route Map to Business Continuity Management, Meeting the Requirements of BS25999*, BSI Business Information Publishing, ISBN-13: 978-0-580-50952-0.

Thejendra BS, (2006) *Disaster Recovery and Business Continuity*, IT Governance Publishing, ISBN-13: 978-1-905356-14-0.

Wright S, (2008), *PCI DSS, A practical guide to implementation*, IT Governance Publishing, ISBN-13: 978-1-905356-45-4.

Zittrain J, (2008), *The Future of the Internet – And How to Stop It*, _www.penguin.com_, ISBN-13: 978-1-8461-4014-3.

Other websites

Become a member of the following groups and read their Journals regularly:

- The Information Systems Security Association *www.issa.org/*
- The Information Systems Audit & Control Association *www.isaca.org/Membership/Professional-Membership/Pages/default.aspx?gclid=CPPPh8_25K0C FUNTfAod8Fs49Q.*

Subscribe to Bruce Schneier's monthly e-mail newsletter, Crypto-Gram available at *www.schneier.com.*

ITG RESOURCES

IT Governance Ltd sources, creates and delivers products and services to meet the real-world, evolving IT governance needs of today's organisations, directors, managers and practitioners.

The ITG website (*www.itgovernance.co.uk*) is the international one-stop-shop for corporate and IT governance information, advice, guidance, books, tools, training and consultancy. On the website you will find the following page related to the subject matter of this book:

www.itgovernance.co.uk/iso27001.aspx.

Publishing Services

IT Governance Publishing (ITGP) is the world's leading IT-GRC publishing imprint that is wholly owned by IT Governance Ltd.

With books and tools covering all IT governance, risk and compliance frameworks, we are the publisher of choice for authors and distributors alike, producing unique and practical publications of the highest quality, in the latest formats available, which readers will find invaluable.

www.itgovernancepublishing.co.uk is the website dedicated to ITGP. Other titles published by ITGP that may be of interest include:

- Nine Steps to Success: An ISO27001:2013 Implementation Overview

  www.itgovernance.co.uk/shop/p-963-nine-steps-to-success-an-iso-270012013-implementation-overview-second-edition.aspx

- CyberWar, CyberTerror, CyberCrime and CyberActivism

www.itgovernance.co.uk/shop/p-511-cyberwar-cyberterror-cybercrime-and-cyberactivism-second-edition.aspx

- Managing Information Security Breaches: Studies from real life

  www.itgovernance.co.uk/shop/p-923.aspx.

We also offer a range of off-the-shelf toolkits that give comprehensive, customisable documents to help users create the specific documentation they need to properly implement a management system or standard. Written by experienced practitioners and based on the latest best practice, ITGP toolkits can save months of work for organisations working towards compliance with a given standard.

For further information please review the following pages:

- ISO27001 2013 ISMS Standalone Documentation Toolkit

  www.itgovernance.co.uk/shop/p-1462.aspx

- Full range of toolkits

  www.itgovernance.co.uk/shop/c-129-toolkits.aspx.

Books and tools published by IT Governance Publishing (ITGP) are available from all business booksellers and the following websites:

www.itgovernance.eu   *www.itgovernanceusa.com*

www.itgovernance.in   *www.itgovernancesa.co.za*

www.itgovernance.asia.

Training Services

IT Governance offers an extensive portfolio of training courses designed to educate information security, IT governance, risk management and compliance professionals. Our classroom and online training programmes will help you develop the skills required to deliver best practice and compliance to your organisation. They will also enhance your career by providing you with industry standard certifications and increased peer recognition. Our range of courses offer a structured learning path from Foundation to Advanced level in the key topics of information security, IT governance, business continuity and service management.

ISO/IEC 27001:2013 is the international management standard that helps businesses and organisations throughout the world develop a best-in-class Information Security Management System (ISMS). Knowledge and experience in implementing and maintaining ISO27001 compliance are considered to be essential to building a successful career in information security. We have the world's first programme of certificated ISO27001 education with Foundation, Lead Implementer, Risk Management and Lead Auditor training courses. Each course is designed to provide delegates with relevant knowledge and skills and an industry-recognised qualification awarded by the International Board for IT Governance Qualifications (IBITGQ).

Full details of all IT Governance training courses can be found at *www.itgovernance.co.uk/training.aspx*.

Professional Services and Consultancy

Your mission to plug critical security gaps will be greatly assisted by IT Governance consultants, who have advised hundreds of information security managers in the adoption of ISO27001 information security management systems (ISMS).

At IT Governance, we understand that information, information security and information technology are always business issues, and not just IT ones. Our consultancy services assist you in managing information security strategies in harmony with business goals, conveying the right messages to your colleagues to support decision-making.

The organisation's assets, security and data systems, not to mention its reputation, are all in your hands. A major security breach could spell disaster. Timely advice and support from IT Governance expert consultants could make all the difference, enabling you to identify risks and put the necessary controls in place before there's a need to respond to a serious incident.

For more information about ISO27001 consultancy from IT Governance Ltd, see:

www.itgovernance.co.uk/consulting.aspx.

Newsletter

IT governance is one of the hottest topics in business today, not least because it is also the fastest moving.

You can stay up to date with the latest developments across the whole spectrum of IT governance subject matter, including; risk management, information security, ITIL and IT service management, project governance, compliance and so much more, by subscribing to ITG's core publications and topic alert emails.

Simply visit our subscription centre and select your preferences: *www.itgovernance.co.uk/newsletter.aspx.*

EU for product safety is Stephen Evans, The Mill Enterprise Hub, Stagreenan, Drogheda, Co. Louth, A92 CD3D, Ireland. (servicecentre@itgovernance.eu)

www.ingramcontent.com/pod-product-compliance
Lightning Source LLC
Chambersburg PA
CBHW060401220326
41598CB00023B/2989